EX-LIBRIS

This Book Presented in Memory of

Mrs. J. W. Taylor
mother of
Mrs. S. E. Harris

Given by

Mr. & Mrs. J. H. Monday

Questions God Asks

Questions God Asks

HUNTER BECKELHYMER

ABINGDON PRESS

NEW YORK • NASHVILLE

QUESTIONS GOD ASKS

Copyright © 1961 by Abingdon Press

Library of Congress Catalog Card Number: 61-5192

Scripture quotations unless otherwise noted are
from the Revised Standard Version of the Bible
and are copyright 1946 and 1952 by the Division
of Christian Education of the National Council
of the Churches of Christ in the U.S.A.

SET UP, PRINTED, AND BOUND BY THE
PARTHENON PRESS, AT NASHVILLE,
TENNESSEE, UNITED STATES OF AMERICA

dedicated to the *members*
of the *Christian Church*
in Hiram, Ohio

Preface

The late Edward Scribner Ames used to say that the finest compliment he ever received on any of his sermons, delivered in the University Church of Disciples of Christ in Chicago, was given him by a sweet little old lady. Gripping his hand as she left morning services there, she said, "Dr. Ames, the things you make me think about are more important than the things you say."

That is a compliment I would here like to pay to Ralph Haas, whose sermon on "The Inquiring God" appeared in *The Pulpit* for November, 1957. Whether or not what I have said here is more important than what he said there, it is at least developed at greater length and in more detail. He may claim whatever credit is to be claimed for sending my mind along the lines of thought presented in these chapters, but he must not be held responsible for what I have presented.

In the same way, I hope that this little book will serve to stimulate other minds to go beyond what is written here in their awareness of God's searching presence in human affairs. The list of questions I have chosen for discussion by no means exhausts those preserved for us in scripture. A volume of equal length and value could surely be made from the questions which Jesus addressed to his hearers. Perhaps someday it will be written, by myself or another who has been made to think of things, if not more important, at least beyond what I have said here. Whether or not another volume appears, this book will have served its purpose if it helps to lead those who read it into a creative meeting with the mind of the heavenly Father. He and they can take it from there.

HUNTER BECKELHYMER

Contents

Questions God Asks

CHAPTER 1

The God Who Inquires

*In the year that King Uzziah died I saw the
Lord sitting upon a throne, high and lifted up;
and his train filled the temple. . . . I heard the
voice of the Lord saying, "Whom shall I send,
and who will go for us?" Then I said, "Here
I am! Send me."* (Isa. 6:1, 8)

God is the answer. We
are assured of that on every hand these days. It is the
theme song of a popular gospel quartet on television.
Indeed it has become a sort of theme song for the whole
country during these years of religion's popularity. We are
all aware that there has been in recent years a growth of
interest in things religious in our land. Its signs are too well
known to need more than brief mention here. Church
membership and attendance are at all time highs, both
numerically and in percentage of the population involved.
Furthermore, this interest is manifest at nearly all levels of
our culture. It is heard in the selections offered on the
jukeboxes in restaurants and bars. It is counted in the
stupendous statistical response to popular revivalists. It is

apparent on the campuses of colleges and universities. It is hinted in the themes of many modern plays, and much current literature. Political and military leaders, and some scientists, have added their voices to those of ministers and evangelists in saying that the solution of mankind's most vexing problems lies at the religious level. God is the answer.

The widespread public awareness is a sound one, that our human predicaments are not to be resolved by tinkering with the symptoms. Bernard Iddings Bell rightly observed that "our disorders are not those of mere housekeeping; it is the whole sewer system that is out of whack." But when we speak of God being the answer we ought to be thinking in terms of God's radical challenge to our notions and habits, not in terms of a few pious decorations being added to business as usual. It is here that the popular turning to religion in our day falls short. There is abundant evidence that some who say that God is the answer think of him as something added at the top, rather than as a foundation. He is tacked *onto,* rather than built *upon.* Too often the assumption seems to be made that God will make our nation strong in the face of her enemies if we invoke his name when announcing our policies. We are led to believe that he will prosper almost any business enterprise that is undertaken with positive thinking. We are assured that God will allay all anxieties and relieve all tensions if he is sought earnestly in prayer. The ultimate in divine cooperation was announced not long ago in the title of a popular columnist's contribution to a daily paper. It proclaimed, "Take God into Partnership for Sound Sleep."

Whether the columnist himself, or the editor, perpetrated that cozy prescription for insomnia, I don't know. I didn't read any further.

One of the ten commandments, familiar to us since childhood, is, "You shall not take the name of the Lord your God in vain." The most common interpretation of this commandment is that it prohibits cussin'. It does. But I feel reasonably sure that God had rather hear a prize fighter emit a heartfelt oath than give him half-credit for his latest victory in the ring. The ultimate profanity is to attribute human successes to God's help which he could have no interest in helping if our Christian understanding of his purposes is a true one. Worse than the casual profanity of rough lips is the calculated profanity of the smooth tongue which invokes the name of the Lord to hallow some viewpoint or enterprise in the formulation of which the divine will was never really sought. We take the Lord's name in vain more often in calling upon him to bless than in calling upon him to damn.

James Luther Adams, now of Harvard Divinity School, used to tell his students of his own school days in New England where a certain brand of boneless codfish fillets are prepared and widely advertised. One day he was taking a walk through the countryside, and as he came over the brow of a hill he saw in the distance a tidy white New England church. From his perspective, a billboard, actually some distance beyond the church, seemed to be perched squarely on top of the roof. It startled him to read what seemed indeed to be a pathetic theology for a Christian church to proclaim to the world—Gorton's God: No Bones.

The good professor made of this little incident a commentary upon the spineless and obliging deity which is too commonly believed in by Christian people. Both are optical illusions.

God, if he be God, cannot be manipulated or bent to our purposes. He is not a symbol, like the British Crown, who puts his seal of approval upon whatever schemes and policies his subjects and ministers devise. He does not lend his blessing, much less his power, to whatever is done in his name. Our danger today is not that we deny God, but that we try to domesticate him. It may help some people to arrive at an awareness of the heavenly Father to empathize with a crooner while he sings "The Man Upstairs," or "My Friend," or "He." But one has not entered fully into the presence of the Eternal until he has felt somewhat as Isaiah felt one day in the temple at Jerusalem. (Things do happen in church sometimes.) Some scholars think that the occasion of the prophet's experience was the Israelite new year's day ceremonies. In them the divine ruler is symbolically escorted to the throne, there to determine the fate of the people in the year ahead. Isaiah, perhaps, was in that semicomatose condition that frequently besets those who are hearing again a familiar liturgy. And then it happened. At just that moment there came to Isaiah the spine-chilling truth—"My God, this is real." Beyond this cultic ceremony and form is the awesome reality of the sovereign God in whose hands the fate of the people does rest indeed.

"I saw the Lord sitting upon a throne, high and lifted up," said Isaiah, writing of his experience later, "and his train filled the temple." The prophet then described other particulars of his vision which were typical of a Hebrew of that day and age. He saw the six-winged seraphim, those imaginary creatures with which the ancients peopled the heavens. Antiphonally they cried, "Holy, holy, holy is the Lord of hosts; the whole earth is full of his glory." And the foundations of the thresholds shook. Isaiah's feeling was that he was undone. He felt himself to be an unclean man living among an unclean people. There followed a progression of awareness in which his sense of guilt and unworthiness gave way to the knowledge of being forgiven and made clean. Then God impaled Isaiah's conscience with a question. "Whom shall I send?" That is, "what do *you* intend to do about it?" It is safe to say that Isaiah did not feel like slapping God on the back, much less taking him into partnership for a sound night of sleep. Indeed, God's pressing inquiry prodded Isaiah out of his comfort, and laid upon him the scratchy mantle of the prophet. He said, "Here I am! Send me." (Isa. 6:1-8.)

God is indeed the answer. He is the ultimate context of our lives here. The whole creation is of his conception and his making. The orderly sequence we know as cause and effect, both in nature and in human affairs, is his design. Our existence is by his plan. Our ambitions and achievements are all by his leave. Moreover, our Christian faith assures us that God loves us. He desires only good for us. His concern for us and his hope for us are unmixed with any malice or duplicity whatsoever. Surely this divine power and wisdom and love are the proper foundations for all our human problem solving, however small or however big. Any plans or policies of ours that do not reckon with the will of God are too narrowly conceived and too shallow in base. They simply are not realistic. On the other hand, the earnest seeking of God's will for us is the way to begin on any problem. Doing his will, insofar as we can ascertain it and carry it through, is surely the sovereign solution to our predicaments and the way to our well-being. In this fundamental sense God is the answer, and the platitude is profoundly true.

But to think of God's name as a magic key to success in whatever we may undertake is both sacrilegious and silly. To think of him as an oracle who will solve for us whatever issues we pose to him in prayer is to misunderstand prayer. For God is quite as apt to create tensions within us as to relieve them, and he is more apt to prevent sleep than to induce it. He who makes us lie down in green pastures also searches out our paths and our lying down until we cry out, "Whither shall I go from thy Spirit, or whither shall I flee from thy presence?" Or as Hosea discovered, sometimes "the Lord has a controversy with the inhabitants of the land" (Hos. 4:1).

If the Bible represents truly the ways of God with men— and I think it does—God not only settles problems; he stirs them up. "Woe to him who seeks to pour oil upon the waters when God has brewed them into a gale," roared Father Mapple to his congregation of New Bedford whalers in Melville's novel, *Moby Dick*. The same observation has been made in different imagery by Charles C. West when he wrote, "We turn (to God) for help when our foundations are shaking, only to learn that it is God who is shaking them." God not only answers questions—he asks them. He not only guides us through basic issues where we are floundering; he guides us into basic issues we had rather ignore. He hovers behind our earthly existence and makes us think about it. He calls to us from the very depths of mystery that surrounds us here, and asks what do you make of it. Or again with abrupt interrogation he brings us face to face with a moral issue we prefer to skirt. He asks a question that evokes from us an acknowledgment of moral responsibility and obliges us to take a stand. By another inquiry he may lead us gently to an insight which we henceforth think we discovered all by ourselves. Some of God's inquiries are imperious, some are plaintive. Some seem harsh and sarcastic, others are infinitely tender. But by them all, as the master counselor, he leads us to a deeper understanding of ourselves and of him. In such inquiries of God the literature of the Bible abounds.

Not many of us, of course, think of God addressing men in audible speech in biblical days or our own—although motion picture makers usually endow him with a sepulchral baritone voice with the aid of an echo chamber. When we read in the scriptures that God spoke to someone, our minds naturally translate it into something other than mouth to ear communication. Perhaps it was the ripening of an insight in a reverent mind. Or the cry of a godly conscience, or the distillation from long observation and divinely disciplined thought. God is able to speak to men through the raptured affirmations of the mystic, and even through the legends of a God-loving people. The divine wisdom has been imparted to men through all of these ways singly and in combination. There is one point in human history, however, where most Christians affirm without hesitation that God's voice became for a while audible. It is in the words of Jesus of Nazareth. In a way too real to doubt and too deep to define he spoke for God with a sureness that none has matched before or since.

The inquiries of God to which we give our attention here are all to be found in the Bible. Some of them are from the oldest legendary material. Some are from the beginnings of historical material. Some are from the literary masterpieces of biblical narrative where the hearer is not the character in the story but the author who wrote it. One is from the mouth of Jesus during his earthly life, and others are from the risen Christ as he addressed the consciousness of the early Church. The questions which are treated here are by no means exhaustive, but they are, I believe representative. It matters very little, as we hear these inquiries again, what part of the Bible they came from, although some knowledge of their setting is of course necessary to grasp what the question is really all about. They are in the Bible because they represent and reflect genuine meetings of God with men in which the Divine Mind did not echo the human mind, but challenged it, probed it, accosted it, stood athwart it. These inquiries have a way of becoming painfully contemporary and embarrassingly relevant however ancient or mythical the material in which they are preserved. Although in their scriptural settings these searching questions were usually addressed to individuals, they leap out of their spots in time and place to meet us today. These questions, whatever their settings in scripture or the hour of their origins in history, represent authentic encounters of the human mind with the Divine Mind. It is because of this that they spring from the pages of scripture to arrange for us today a meeting in which we are searched and known.

CHAPTER 2

Where Are You?

And they heard the sound of the Lord God walking in the garden in the cool of the day, and the man and his wife hid themselves from the presence of the Lord God among the trees of the garden. But the Lord God called to the man, and said to him, "Where are you?"
(Gen. 3:8-9)

The story of Adam and Eve is a myth. But what *is* a myth? Is it a fairy story told for the amusement of children? Is it an old wives' tale passed on from generation to generation—interesting perhaps, but taken seriously only by the ignorant? Is myth merely another name for an ancient superstition? Is it an outright lie, meant to deceive? Is it just folk lore—harmless enough, but of no value to an age that plots its course by the certitudes of science? Is myth another name for legend —quaint survivals from some unsophisticated era of our human past whose value, if any, is purely literary? These are the ideas that usually come to mind when we hear the word "myth."

Actually myths have served an important role in human history. They are bearers of human insight into the ultimate nature of the world in which they live. Myths have sent men into battle and stirred them to adventure and exploration. Some myths have aroused men to achievement, and some have discouraged all effort. Some have ennobled human living, and some have degraded it. We must judge them not as true or false—since by definition they are all "false" in the purely factual sense. We must judge them rather by the spirit they engender and the behavior they evoke. Henry Nelson Wieman used to tell this story to illustrate the uses of myth in human affairs. Some of the American Indians were discovered to be planting a lively little fish in each hill of their corn. Their explanation of this excellent bit of progressive agriculture was that the spirit of the fish entered into the spirit of the corn, and made it grow tall and produce abundantly. One would hardly call this myth a fairy story, a superstition, a tall tale, or a lie. Actually it was the attempt of a childlike people to explain some realities of life. The fact is that it does wonders for a hill of corn to have a little good, rich fertilizer planted with it. We moderns wouldn't explain things exactly as the Indians did; we recognize their explanation to be mythical. Yet it helped those people into a very sound and fruitful relationship with reality. It increased their crops.

All this is by way of making our minds receptive to the value of the Adam and Eve story even while recognizing it as entirely mythical. Though one may, and does, discount as fact every particular of the story—Adam, the creation of Eve from his rib, the mysterious tree, the garden, the

21

snake—one can see the story as it has been conceived and preserved for us to be a vehicle of truth. Through it we may indeed come into the presence of the Divine Mind, and enter into a healing and redeeming relationship with him who made us. Indeed, this ancient myth which pictures man as a special creation of God who succumbed to a distinctively human level of temptation is more relevant to our human condition than some of our more modern myths which picture man as a complicated machine or a sophisticated ape. Our grasp of reality is not so sure even in this twentieth century that we can despise any insight into the ways of God with men, however ancient. We function by some deadly modern myths and ridiculous superstitions of our own. It is well to turn again to a Bible story we heard as children, but which challenges our thinking and behavior as adults. From the inspired lore of an ancient people, a particular ancient people, we moderns are brought up short by an authentic inquiry from the living God.

The story begins with God's creation of the world. (Gen. 4:7.) There is purpose behind creation. It is the work of a good God. The whole and all of its parts are good in conception and intent. There is order and meaning and design to it. Then God made man from the dust of the earth. That is to say, man is a part of nature, and one with it. He is made of the same elements as the soil, the trees, and all living things. He is a child of nature. But man is special too. Of all the creatures which God made it is said of man alone that God personally breathed into his nostrils the breath of life. Then God prepared a special place for man—a garden spot. He filled it with every tree that gives food to eat, and every tree that is lovely to behold. He placed man in the midst of a pleasant and provident earth. He gave man all he needed for a full life—food for his body and food for his soul. Moreover, he was to have work to do. He was to till the garden, and keep it. He was to cultivate it, manage it, care for it as it cared for him. The earth was to be enjoyed in all of its goodness through man's faithfulness and obedience. The whole arrangement was provident and benign, designed for human well-being and joy.

But arbitrarily, as is God's right, man was denied the fruit of one tree. No explanation was given him; it was a simple commandment. We parents do not—indeed we can not—explain every command that we make to our children. Some day when they are mature enough we may explain the command, and when they are responsible enough we may revoke it. But childhood, in the individual or in the race, makes necessary some arbitrary limitations of freedom. Perhaps here the story indicates this fact of life in this pictorial fashion. There are limits to man's rights—limits beyond which God does not mean man to push his knowledge or his power. A student at Atlanta University once asked Charles Leander Hill, president of Wilburforce University, what he thought of the discovery of atomic power. The Negro educator's answer was a modern restatement of the fact which man has known about himself at least as long as the Eden story has been known: "It's bad to know what God knows and not be like God is."

Then the Lord God said, "It is not good that the man should be alone; I will make him a helper fit for him." So, the story continues, God began to make all kinds of crea-

23

tures. He brought each one in turn to Adam to see what the man thought of them. Adam wasn't much interested. The bored or casual sound he made when each was showed to him became the name of that animal. That's how the animals got their names. But none of these was a suitable companion and helper for man. So God put Adam into a deep sleep. He took a part of Adam's own body and from it fashioned a woman, a being like man himself. When God showed her to Adam, his interest picked up at once. He exclaimed the ancient equivalent of "now you're cooking." ("This is the stroke" is the literal translation from Hebrew of Adam's comment.) This is absolutely *it*, was Adam's reaction. Bone of my bones, and flesh of my flesh. Again the story makes its affirmation of the inherent rightness of Creation.

But now enters the counter theme, the dark note, the shadow of tragedy in paradise. A part of the creation is rebellious. There is disaffection in the created world. There is counter purpose and disobedience. The whole situation is still experimental and not quite stable. The universe is made, but not completely under control. Parts of it are still wild and unsubdued to the Maker's will. And all this rebellion is personified in a serpent.

The serpent made his play through the woman. He started by misrepresenting things. "Tsk, tsk," he said to Eve, "all this wonderful fruit, and God won't let you eat any of it." But Eve corrected him quickly, saying that they could eat any and all that they wanted except from the one tree. She added that God had forbidden that tree to them, with the warning that if they touched it they would die.

24

"Oh ho," said the serpent in effect, "you won't die. Don't you see what God is doing to you? He's exploiting you. He wants to keep you in ignorance and subjection. Do you know *why* God won't let you eat the fruit of that tree? It will open your eyes. It will make you as smart as he is. He doesn't want you to be on a level with him, that's all. Get wise. That is quite a tree." (I don't know who started the idea that the tree that caused the trouble in Eden was an apple tree. There is no apple mentioned in the Bible story. One commentator advanced the theory that the fruit that caused all the difficulty was a green pear. The symbolic nature of the whole story is nowhere more obvious than in the identification of this tree as the tree of the knowledge of good and evil.)

Under the serpent's subtle insinuations, the fruit began to look mighty good to Eve. It looked good to eat, which fact she hadn't noticed before, for they had plenty. More important, it would advance one's status in the world, indeed make one like God himself. Notice that evil did not enter by way of the physical appetites, such as hunger, lust, or love of comfort and ease. It entered by way of the mind and the spirit. The serpent knew which nerves to tickle to corrupt a man and woman, and to undo the harmony of God's creation. He appealed to their pride, to their vanity, to their ambition. He sought to make them feel wronged. He told them they were cheated, that they were being exploited. This was all that was necessary to make them forget every joy, every privilege, every blessing that was theirs, and to reach out for the prerogatives of divinity until they crashed in a heap. The serpent didn't fiddle

25

around trying to make human beings play dog; he tempted them to play God. That is the way evil made its pitch. And it worked. Adam and Eve ate the fruit, not in ignorance but in rebellion. Not from need, but from ambition.

The consequences were instantaneous and disasterous. Their eyes were opened, if not to the full range of good and evil at least to the fact of sex. Their embarrassment at their nakedness represents an estrangement from the nature of which they were a part. They made pitiful gestures of covering their bodies, which very act betrayed them. They felt shame. They felt guilt. They knew fear for the first time. Strangers now in their own home, alienated from their Maker, they tried to hide themselves from his presence —to prevent or postpone any meeting with God when they heard him in the garden in the cool of the day.

Then it was that God sought out the man by calling to him *"Where are you?"* We cannot imagine God being unaware of where man was. We can imagine God wanting man to become fully aware of where he was, and why. "Where are you? Not out walking through the garden in the cool of the day, enjoying its beauties and the natural pleasures it affords. Not busy about your task of subduing nature to your use. Not planning with eagerness for your descendants. Not enjoying the company of each other as I meant you to do, but accusing and counteraccusing." We can well imagine Adam reminding Eve for the rest of their lives that it was her nosiness that got them into trouble. And Eve would reply that if Adam were any kind of a husband, he would know when not to let her have what she wanted. And their little boys, Cain and Abel, would listen to their parents' bitter quarrels.

Worst of all was Adam's fear of meeting the God who gave him life and opportunity. The man and woman were avoiding him who was their friend, their health, and their peace. They were cowering in fear when they should have been walking in dignity. They were hiding in shame when they were meant to be standing in confidence. And why? Not because of their weakness, but because of their presumption. Not for seeking knowledge, but for grabbing at power. Not because they were mere humans, but because they sought to make themselves into gods. Not because of their mistakes, but because of their rebellion. And the Lord God called to the man, and said to him, "Where are you?"

How that question searches us out today, cringing in fear as we are in the midst of a potential paradise. It asks us to wake up to where we are, and why we are there. It is addressed to a generation of men who have tried to avoid God, and who now shiver in terror in a world made hostile and threatening by their own disobedience. Inexorably it seeks out those who have alienated themselves from their Maker by a rebellious spirit—those who presume to be self-made men, or who aspire to be—those who seek power over the lives of themselves and others that men are not meant to have—all those who who would play the role of God in the affairs of the world—all those who through their own ambition become gods to themselves and who aspire to be gods to other men—all those who in sullenness or anger at their human lot overreach themselves. It is in these things that the very harmony of the created world is

27

disrupted and the benign purposes of our Maker delayed. It is in these things that we become estranged not only from God but from our neighbors, our brothers, and ourselves. The Divine is in every impulse that leads us to face squarely where we are, and why.

But this inquiry of God is not altogether ominous. It is also infinitely tender. It affirms unmistakably that God cares where we are. In the Eden story, the Creator didn't make man and woman to put them in the garden and abandon them there forever. He made them for fellowship with himself. The story pictures God returning to the garden in the cool of the day to walk with his creatures in fellowship and love. He came to be with them, and for them to be with him each day. And when he found man alienated from him by his sin, he called to him in loving concern. God asks where we are because he cares where we are. He seeks us in sadness more than in anger; in purposes redemptive more than in punitive.

Indeed, said Jesus, it is not the father's will that one of his children should perish. When he calls "Where are you," the pronoun is always singular. We have not really heard it until we have heard it addressed to us individually, intimately, and insistently. Theodore F. Adams tells a story, perhaps well-known, about an official government census taker at work in Scotland. He knocked on the door of one home where there was quite obviously a large family, and the mother opened the door. After learning that both parents were living, the census taker inquired how many children there were. The mother replied, "well, there's Mary and Brucie and Elizabeth and James and—"

"No, no," replied the man, "not the names, just the number."

"Well, there's Mary and Brucie and Elizabeth and James and—"

"Just the number please," insisted the exasperated census taker.

"Och," replied the mother, "I dinna think o' the numbers; I think o' the bairns."

So with God. Jesus said, "If a man has a hundred sheep, and one of them has gone astray, does he not leave the ninety-nine on the hills and go in search of the one that went astray? And if he finds it, truly, I say to you, he rejoices over it more than over the ninety-nine that never went astray. So it is not the will of my Father who is in heaven that one of these little ones should perish." (Matt. 18:12-14.) Neither a little lamb nor a scarred old ram.

Earth is no Eden today. Indeed the Eden of perfect harmony and the man of pristine innocence are but a legendary stage setting for a symbolic interpretation of man's woes and responsibilities in a world that yields abundance only to toil, and in which our moral victories are often little more than stand-offs with the serpent. In such a world, we reply to God's inquiry by assuming our responsibilities and commitments with humility and with awareness of need.

James Gould Cozzens caught this in his novel *By Love Possessed*, which is the story of a Christian attorney, Arthur Winner. Winner is mature, responsible, fair-minded, and respected. But in a twenty-four hour period, his stable personal world nearly falls apart completely. An old sin from his own past rises to plague him fresh and keen. Then a

routine lawsuit blows up in his face through a miscalcula-
tion on his part—the defendant runs away. The defendant's
sister, Winner's secretary and personal friend, takes her life
in shame and fear. Then the attorney learns that the senior
partner in the law firm is short some $200,000 in trust
funds under his care. Arthur had the choice of keeping
quiet and giving the old man his outside chance to recoup
the loss, or bringing down several respected families and
institutions, including his own, in financial and moral ruin.
Shaken and chastened, he decides to keep his mouth shut
and carry on the best he can with what remains of his
honor, skill, judgment, and good intentions. The book ends
as he calls at his old home where his aged mother and
aunt, also his responsibilities, now live. "Arthur," called
Aunt Maud from upstairs upon hearing someone enter the
house, "are you there?" We catch a clearer glimpse of a
mature man's response to his place in this world in the
weary attorney's reply: "I'm here," he gravely assured the
crochety old lady.[1]

We're here. The Eden story of man's disobedience and
rebellion is not the complete picture of evil in our world.
After all, Adam didn't make the serpent! Adam rather
timidly voiced the human protest we feel to taking all the
blame even for our own sins. His reply to God was, in
effect, that God had given him a wife and when she
offered him the fruit he assumed that it had God's approval.
This is a risky assumption, but enough to state the theme

[1] New York: Harcourt, Brace and Co., 1957.

30

that there are other factors besides man's own cussedness in his sinning.

Thomas Mann stated this rather daringly in his retelling of the story of Joseph in Egypt. Joseph is aware that his spectacular rise to power was not solely of his own doing, yet he has a guilty conscience about it. "That's just it," muses Joseph. "Man bears God's guilt; and it would be no more than right if one day God were to make up his mind to bear our guilt. How he, the holy and blameless, could do that is hard to say. I should think he would need to become a man to that end." [2]

He *did!* But that is another story.

[2] *Joseph in Egypt* (New York: Alfred A. Knopf, Inc., 1938), I, 356.

CHAPTER 3

Where Is Your Brother?

Cain said to Abel his brother, "Let us go out to the field." And when they were in the field, Cain rose up against his brother Abel, and killed him. Then the Lord said to Cain, "Where is Abel your brother?" He said, "I do not know; am I my brother's keeper?"
(Gen. 4:8-9)

However insistently God may search out the individual conscience to make it answer for itself, he does not stop there. The story of Adam and Eve does not end with their eviction from Eden. It continues into another generation. The first sons of Adam and Eve were Cain and Abel. Cain became a farmer; Abel was a shepherd. Apparently farmers and stockmen couldn't get along any better in the Middle East than they could in the Middle West. Their antagonisms were as sharp along the Tigris and Euphrates as they were later along the Cimarron, Republican, and Red. Anyhow a rivalry arose between these two legendary brothers because of their different occupations. For some reason Abel's efforts received the smile of heaven, and Cain's didn't. Therefore Cain became hurt, mad, envious, jealous. Of course Cain had considerable provocation, but life is full of provocations. And the writer of the story goes to considerable pains to make clear that Cain's efforts would be equally acceptable to heaven if he did equally well in his own way. (Gen. 4:7.) But this did not suffice for Cain whose envy of his brother festered in his heart. He coaxed Abel out to look over the back forty, and when he got him out there he killed him. Then it was that the Lord demanded of Cain, "Where is Abel your brother?"

Now Cain, whatever else he was, was a "realist." There was no "fuzzy-headed liberalism" about him. There was no "sentimental idealism" or "do-goodism" in his make up. He knew that if he didn't look out for his interests, no one else would do it for him. He looked after number one, and he expected everyone else to look after himself. It was his policy to do the other fellow before the other fellow did him. So the question put to Cain was alien to his way of thinking and pinpointed to his sin, as inquiries from God inevitably are: "Where is your brother?"

Cain's reaction showed that the inquiry had scored. "How should I know," he snapped, in effect. "That is not my affair. That is his worry. Am I my brother's keeper?" Cain not only lied, he repudiated the idea that he should be *expected* to know or care where his brother was. But God pressed in. "What have you done? The voice of your brother's blood is crying to me from the ground. . . . When you till the ground, it shall no longer yield to you its strength; you shall be a fugitive and a wanderer upon the

33

earth" (Gen. 4:9-12). The implications of God's intercourse with Cain are that men *are* responsible for each other. Not only does God ask me where I am, and my brother where he is. He also asks me where my brother is, and he asks my brother where I am. Not only does God himself care where every last one of my brothers is—he expects me to care. And he expects my brothers to care where I am.

From the very beginning of history, men have been trying to live by the philosophy of Cain. Deep rifts have opened between men because of their respective economic fortunes. Some seem to have enjoyed the prospering smile of heaven, and others have not. If that sounds fortuitous and arbitrary, it is. Think how much we Americans owe to the fact that we have had the use of a rich virgin continent, rather than a few rocky islands, or a penurious desert, or a land long since used up or depleted. The wife of an Indian physician once told me that at their hospital in India they saved every incoming letter that the hospital or its staff received. They used the paper to wrap up pills when they gave them to the patients. And when the patient returned for more medicine, if the prescription was the same, the same paper was used over again a second time—and a third. Here in America one of our domestic problems is to dispose of second-class mail, waste paper, cardboard boxes, cellophane, foil, and other packaging materials, fast enough to keep from being buried alive in them. Let this single contrast suffice to indicate the incredible difference in living standards between the United States and most of the rest of the world. There is little wonder that we are envied. There is even less wonder that we are cordially disliked, particularly when we act as though our high standard of living were due exclusively to our superior virtue, intelligence, or economic system. There is no doubt that Abel was the victim in the Bible story, in that he was murdered. But maybe justifiable homicide would have been a fairer indictment of Cain. Maybe Abel was so insufferably smug that anyone would have felt like choking him!

Be that as it may, economic rifts are deep ones. Rebecca McCann noted a relatively minor instance:

> No other two people can ever have
> Such different points of view
> As the man who sublets a furnished flat
> And the tenant he rents it to.[1]

It is probable that the rivalry of Cain and Abel in the Bible story reflected a rivalry between the herd-raising Hebrews and the grain-raising farmers of Canaan in the days of Israel's conquest of Canaan. And it is no joke that that same rivalry was echoed in the range wars between farmers and cattlemen in America. It appeared also in the War between the States which found Northern businessmen pitted against Southern plantation owners, as well as abolitionists against the defenders of slavery as such, and federalists against states righters. Economic classes are real, and economic rifts are deep, even within America itself.

And what chasms have opened between men because of the different pigmentation of their skins, and the different folding of their eyelids.

[1] From *Complete Cheerful Cherub* by Rebecca McCann. Copyright 1932 by Covici, Friede, Inc. Copyright 1960 by Crown Publishers, Inc. Used by permission of the publishers.

> Millions and millions of mankind
> Burned, crushed, broken, mutilated,
> Slaughtered, and for what? For thinking!
> For walking round the world in the wrong
> Skin, the wrong-shaped noses, eyelids:
> Living at the wrong address—
> London, Berlin, Hiroshima,
> Wrong night, wrong city.
> There never could have been so many
> Suffered more for less.[2]

It makes our race troubles here in America neither better nor worse, morally, to note that physical differences that are really quite insignificant have been used in nearly every age and every land as a pretext for depriving men and women and children of privileges, livelihood, and often life itself.

In our day, the whole world is becoming polarized around two great world powers—the United States and Russia. Economic differences are part of it. The race issue enters into it more than we like to think. Raw nationalism fans the flames. Russia's imperial ambitions are the largest single source of trouble, but the stark fear which rival military establishments inevitably have for each other is not far behind. Although not many individual citizens would murder their brothers in cold blood, nations will do that very thing. They will cut off each other's livelihood, and drop bombs on each other in the night. For that matter, decent men and women will do all manner of cruel things as groups, and through their organizations and institutions,

[2] Archibald MacLeish, *J.B.*, Act I (New York: Houghton Mifflin Co. 1959).

that they would not dream of doing to each other as individuals. As Arnold Toynbee put it:

Bad behaviour that would be condemned unhesitatingly by the conscience of an individual culprit is apt to be condoned when it is perpetrated by Leviathan [the nation], under the illusion that the first person is absolved from self-centeredness by being transposed from the singular number into the plural. This is, however, just the opposite of the truth; for, when an individual projects his self-centeredness on to a community, he is able, with less sense of sin, to carry his egotism to greater lengths of enormity. "Patriotism is the last refuge of a scoundrel" [Dr. Johnson in Boswell's *Life*] and the callousness of committees testifies still more eloquently than the fury of mobs that, in collective action, the ego is capable of descending to depths to which it does not fall when it is acting on its individual responsibility.[3]

It is while we are in this condition that we are now engaged in a headlong race to project our enmities from the earth into outer space itself, there to continue them on a grander battlefield with costlier weapons.

> Between us silence stretches far,
> My brother, oh my brother.
> How can we hail a distant star
> Who cannot speak each other? [4]

The Lord said to Cain, "Where is your brother?" And

[3] *An Historian's Approach to Religion* (New York: Oxford University Press, 1956), p. 34.
[4] Elizabeth Burrowes, "Misunderstanding," *The Christian Century*, March 5, 1958.

in the riven relationships of our tortured humanity God addresses that same question to us. Where is your brother in his search for a decent human life, and in his efforts to feed and shelter himself and his family? How is your brother making out in his search for the technical knowledge that will open to him the gates of plenty, and for the deeper knowledge that will give meaning to his life and efforts? Can your brother read and write? Why not? Where is your brother in his struggle to gain the dignity, and rights, and opportunities which you daily enjoy? Where is your brother finding sympathy and friendship, if he is? At what strange idolatrous altars does your brother bow; before what god or gods does he prostrate himself? If these questions do not haunt us, they must. For they are addressed to all men by the Father of all men.

Suppose, like Cain, we say, "How should I know? That's his business, not mine. Am I my brother's keeper? I believe in live and let live. I believe in enlightened self-interest. I have nothing against the Negro so long as he stays out of my neighborhood. I want the Japanese people to live, just so their products don't compete with American-made things. I want world peace, but we don't dare negotiate with the Russians while they're ahead in the armaments race, and when we're ahead we don't have to negotiate. I believe in the work of the church, but not in the foreign missions end of it. (There's plenty to do right here at home.)" Suppose our answers be such as these. Can we not hear the judgment of the Eternal—with a vertical orange cloud for an exclamation point—"Henceforth when you till the ground it shall no longer yield to you its

38

strength. You shall be a fugitive and a wanderer upon the earth."

What must we do to be saved? We must accept now, if we have not yet done so, that we *are* our brother's keeper. It has always been true. Men haven't always recognized it as true, and that is one reason there have been so many fugitives and wanderers in human history. Today the world in which we live cannot and will not tolerate any other attitude. It is all too vitally interdependent. Self-interest—in the usual sense of that term—is suicide. National interest—in the usual sense of that term—is sure doom. The Talmud, long ago, illustrated this truth with the following salty parable: "In a boat at sea, one of the men began to bore a hole in the bottom of the boat. On being remonstrated with, he answered, 'I am only boring under my own seat.' 'Yes,' said his comrades, 'but when the sea rushes in we shall all be drowned with you.'" Arnold Toynbee brings it pointedly up to date when he observed: "Our wickedness is not more wicked, and our goodness not more good, than the conduct of our pre-industrial forefathers was. But the practical consequences of our actions, whether bad or good, are now far more serious." [5]

It is literally true that our own interests and the interests of our brothers in the long run are essentially the same. America's health and the health of the world are inseparable. Simon Doniger tells a poignant story about a little girl who participated with her class in a large city school in an air-raid drill. Apparently even a child knows enough

[5] Toynbee, *op. cit.*, p. 153.

of the weapons of our day to realize what a pitiful gesture toward survival an air-raid drill is. Upon returning home she pleaded with her mother, "Mama, can't we go somewhere where there isn't any sky." No, dear, we can't go somewhere where there isn't any sky.

That we are our brother's keeper is more than an inescapable fact and a moral obligation, however. It is also a potential blessing. God means us to accept responsibility for others not only to save our skins, but for the good of our souls. Bearing one another's burdens is not simply an expedient for survival—it is the way to a life infinitely richer than we know. Cain needs Abel not just as a customer for his produce, nor his good will just to avoid costly and dangerous warfare. Cain needs Abel in order to be fully Cain. So, too, you and I are lifted out of our pettiness and triviality by the breadth and depth of our relationships with those who share this earthly life with us. God gave Cain and Abel to each other. And their relationships to each other, their mutual responsibilities and shared enthusiasms, were meant to be a rewarding thing to them both. So, too, the neighbor next door, the strange and unpleasant peoples in another part of town, indeed the very enemy at our gate are not just problems to be solved. They are opportunities for us to become more fully human, and whether they know it or not we are the same opportunities for them.

Thus it is that God's inquiry, "Where is your brother?" adds a deeper dimension to the most commonplace activities of life. Nearly everything we do affects our brother in some way. We are not, therefore, the futile nonentities that we sometimes feel ourselves to be when we confront the baffling complexities of world affairs. We are participants in a perpetual drama in which Abel is embraced or slain, and Cain is correspondingly enriched or impoverished. The votes by which we endorse or protest our leaders' policies, the stocks we select to invest our money in, the jobs at which we work, the publications we strengthen by our subscriptions, the letters we write or don't write to our senators, the organizations to which we pay dues and the resolutions they pass, the opinions we express or don't express, challenge or don't challenge—through all these things our personal lives weigh in the balances, and our brother is lifted up or beaten down by our hand.

Where is your brother? When we hear the divine question and take unto ourselves the responsibilities it implies, life is complicated perhaps, but it also takes on meanings and excitement where only habit and routine would otherwise reign. We are impelled to find out about our brother —what he wants, what he loves, what he fears, what he laughs at, what makes him cry. We become curious and concerned about the ramifications of our own attitudes and behavior and their effects upon him. Indeed whenever God gets through to a man with this question, that man has been led to take the first step toward understanding the infinitely varied human family with whom he must live if he is to live at all. With understanding comes the possibility, and perhaps the impulse, to love his neighbor as he loves himself. And that, said Jesus, is second only to loving God, and with it sums up the law and the prophets.

CHAPTER 4

What Do You See?

*He showed me: behold, the Lord was standing
beside a wall built with a plumb line, with a
plumb line in his hand. And the Lord said to
me, "Amos, what do you see?" And I said, "A
plumb line." Then the Lord said, "Behold, I
am setting a plumb line in the midst of my
people Israel."* (Amos 7:7)

The inquiries of God
are never trivial. They may be sharp, they may be gentle,
they may be embarrassing, they are always searching. They
are never trivial or irrelevant. One such inquiry was heard
and preserved for us by a shepherd who lived in Tekoa
around 750 B.C. Tekoa was a hilltop village about six miles
south of Bethlehem. The shepherd's name was Amos.
Tekoa was not an important village, and Amos was not a
prominent man. He spent his days watching sheep. Probably they were his own, but he had to supplement his income by harvesting the fruit of the sycamore tree. This
fruit was no great delicacy, but poor people ate it. One
day, the word of the Lord came to Amos—of all people—

asking "Amos, what do you see?" That is, "You have eyes; you have a mind; you have been nourished in the religious tradition and the faith of Israel; how do things look to you?"

Here was a man of humble means and of limited opportunities for formal learning, if any. Here was a laboring man far from the centers of culture and power in his day. His rank among the people of his day was modest indeed. He had no connections. He was utterly lacking influence in either the formal or informal ways in which it is exercised. Yet to him came the divine command to assess the life of his hour and place. He heard with the inner hearing of the mind the divine imperative that he render a moral judgment upon the culture in which he lived, based upon his own observation and understanding of it, and against the background of the finest that was in it—its covenant with God. It was a profoundly important question that Amos heard the Lord ask him. It was a deeply disturbing question. It was an extremely revealing question. On it hung the hope of a people's self-criticism, self-correction, and renewal—the capacity of a common man to see his day and age in the perspective of its religious heritage and the present imperatives of the eternal God. That Amos should then have the fiber and courage of a prophet to speak upon what he saw is of course equally important, or even more so. But that is another story. The first issue was whether his perceptions were clear and true, undistorted by considerations of his own convenience and his own involvement in the affairs which he was called upon to assess. "Amos, what do you *see*?" The question is perpetually addressed to every man in every place and every time by the same source of righteousness who addressed it to the shepherd of Tekoa. It takes your measure and mine.

This divine inquiry, for one thing, reveals how far we are able to transcend our circumstances, how far we are able to rise above our surroundings, how well we are able to detach our vision from our situation. It reveals what one is able to see beyond what he could normally be expected to see, and beyond what others want him to see. Notice that the divine inquiry is not "What do the neighbors think?" God does not ask us what Fulton Lewis, Jr. says, nor Drew Pearson. He does not ask us what the Gallup poll reveals. The question is "What do *you* see?"

All of us, of course, are immersed in our own culture. Indeed, all men are immersed in a culture of some sort. And from their culture they acquire a perspective on life; from it they absorb a sense of values. It was tremendously difficult, we may be sure, for Amos to transcend his particular circumstances. It may be even more difficult—or at least more complicated—for us to transcend ours. For instance, most of us were born among that minority of the human race whose skins happen to be white. (Is it ever possible for a white man to see our world scene objectively, much less as a black man must see it?) We were born in that portion of the world where, thanks to Christian traditions, human life is valued. We were born on a continent that rewards our labors with incredible bounty. We were born in a young nation at the hour of its ascendancy and power. We were born in an age of proliferating technology. We are residents of a culture that is enthusiastically and evangelistically commercial. These factors shape our thinking in hundreds of subtle and pervasive ways, and largely determine our sense of values. It is extremely difficult to think critically about them; it is hard work. It is much easier and more natural to take it all for granted and accept it all as it is.

Few of us have any fundamental doubts about that complex of manners and privileges which we call "The American Way of Life." The ambition of most of us is to find a comfortable niche in it, and settle down. If we have a quarrel with it at all, it is apt to be that our niche is not big enough. Wilma Dykeman has written a telling article "The Man in the Grey Flannel Sheet" which illuminates this issue. In it she quotes a young Southern matron who is refreshingly frank on a touchy subject:

I'm sick to death of cocktail party liberals. . . . People who wouldn't dream of being different in their own little circle, of ordering bourbon and water if the boss had set the pace at dry martinis, these organization men ask you with real amazement why more Southerners don't "speak out" on racial matters. Well, some day I'm going to tell them. It's simple. We like to be executive vice-presidents too! [1]

It is simple. Distressingly simple. We are at ease in Zion and we like it that way. Or, as C. S. Lewis once described the process, we think that we are finding our place in the world when in reality the world is finding its place in us. It is Robert Hamill who spelled the process out as it takes place in the lives of many young men. He tells the story of

[1] *The Progressive,* Feb. 1959, p. 8.

a boy named Hank on the campus of a Midwestern university.

Hank's father died when he was a youngster. Hank had to be a bellhop to support his mother and sister. He knew the rough, raw edges of life, and he early resolved to try to remake the business world so its competitive knives would not cut so deep, and its opportunities would be distributed more justly. Everyone called Hank a radical. He didn't adjust to college life. After graduation he got a job. One night under the stars he proposed to a girl; they were his lucky stars, for she was the boss's daughter. That put Hank in the front office where he no longer sees the frayed collars on men's coats or hears the janitor's youngsters beg for things their father's pay check can't buy. Hank has arrived. He owns a bungalow with green shutters and drives a convertible coupé. He thinks American economy is sound. It treats men justly. He has tamed his dreams and has conformed to the pattern of success. He is well adjusted now.[2]

But when God asks us, as continually he does, "What do you see," the stock answers and the party line will not do. No stock answers, no party line, will do. He wants the response of one man's open-eyed vision, one man's disciplined mind, one man's throbbing conscience. When God asked Amos, that was Amos' response. (I realize that in a strict sense, Amos was not judging his own neighborhood of Judea, but a neighboring country—somewhat like a Northerner today criticizing the South. But he was speaking to a common culture from a common religious tradition, and in the name of the one God whom both recognized.

[2] *Gods of the Campus* (Nashville: Abingdon Press, 1949), p. 122.

Certainly the Hebrew prophets as a group, of whom Amos is representative, were deeply involved in the very events to which they addressed themselves. A prophet is not really a prophet except in his own country.) When God asked Amos what he saw, Amos replied, "a plumb line." Amos had probably seen a number of plumb lines in use by a number of masons and carpenters during his lifetime. But on this occasion it became to him a sign and a symbol of God's testing of his people. It was the civilization of which Amos was a part being subjected to the divine standard and measured by it. It was men's works—their building, their devices, their values tested by the true vertical, the true perpendicular, true righteousness and justice. And Amos saw a people out of plumb, crooked and dishonest. He saw them athwart the moral law, and doomed to fall.

On another occasion, or perhaps it was the same one, God asked the question again. This time Amos saw a basket of summer fruit. To the prophetic mood of his mind it represented the approaching end of his people. We don't see the connection here, but an ancient Hebrew would. The word for "summer fruit" and the word for "end" are very much alike in the Hebrew language. Amos couched his insight in an outrageous pun which doesn't come off in English. The point of it was that Israel was overripe, mushy with corruption, and about done for. Amos saw it, and said it (Amos 8:1-3).

Robert Frost wrote a poem in which he suggests an epitaph for his life. In it he calls himself one who engaged his whole lifetime in a "lover's quarrel with the world."

Lover's quarrels are pointed and fundamental, but their aim is to build and not to destroy. They are conducted in loyalty, and look toward reconciliation. Frost has engaged in a life-long lover's quarrel with the world. He has achieved a measure of transcendence of his neighborhood and his culture. He has spoken to it from his own mind and conscience. That is what God's question is all about. "What do you see," the Divine Presence asks us. God knows what our neighbors think. That is between him and them. He knows what the rival groups of scientists think about the continued pollution of the planet through testing nuclear weapons. But what do you think? (Incidentally, the differing viewpoints of government and nongovernment scientists on this issue suggests that something more than science is necessary to free men's vision from their circumstances). God knows the position of our secretary of state on the matter of China's place in the community of nations. But what do you think? He knows the respective viewpoints of the National Association of Manufacturers and of the C.I.O. on matters of labor legislation. But what do you see? The haunting, brooding presence of the Eternal prods us to look beyond the pat answers of our own culture, our own class, and our own day. He dangles plumb lines before our eyes in the midst of our own institutions and habits and those of the world about us. And he asks each individual of us what he sees, and what he has to say. Josiah Gilbert Holland's familiar prayer, "God Give Us Men," if we personalize it into "God *make* us men," is the prayer for us all:

48

God, give us men! A time like this demands
Strong minds, great hearts, true faith, and willing hands;
  Men whom the lust of office does not kill;
Men whom the spoils of office cannot buy;
  Men who possess opinions and a will;
Men who have honor; men who will not lie;
Men who can stand before a demagogue
  And damn his treacherous flatteries without winking!
Tall men, sun-crowned, who live above the fog
  In public duty and private thinking.

Let no one belittle "opinions"—his own or anyone else's. Not all opinions are good ones, of course. And it is ridiculous to think that one man's opinion is as good as another's. But every man's opinions are a reasonably sure indication of his character, and of his basic orientation toward God and the world in which he lives. It is nice to know that a candidate for public office loves dogs, teaches a Sunday-school class, had a good war record, and doesn't beat his wife. But it is infinitely more important to know what his opinions are upon the public issues he will participate in deciding, for such issues are rarely free from moral considerations of the profoundest import. We ought to know from our leaders, "How does it look to you?"

A second import of the divine inquiry, "What do you see?" is that it reveals what we are inwardly. A cartoon in the *New Yorker* a few years ago showed two men in a panel truck driving through the majestic redwoods of one of our Western national parks. The lettering on the truck indicated that it belonged to a company of tree servicers and surgeons. Said the driver to his companion, "This would be

49

a nice account to have." One of the surest principles of psychology is that perception is selective. We see only a portion of what is around us; we see what we are looking for. What we see indicates not only our training and our circumstances, but our loves, our desires, our fears, our faith —in short our inner selves. This is the principle of the famous Rorschach tests, in which the patient is shown a number of seemingly random and nondescript ink blots on white paper. He is asked to tell the psychologist what they look like to him, from which information the psychologist derives insights into the person's character and problems. It doesn't do any good to cheat, because the psychologist knows how to interpret the different varieties of cheating.

But God was using such a test millenniums before psychology became a science. He used it on Amos, and he uses it on us. The world and the experiences of life come to us as a series of consecutive sensations and confusing squiggles until we bring to them some kind of unifying faith. The physical world is a hodge-podge to a child or a savage. But the scientist brings to it the faith that it is knowable—that it is "fit for human intelligence"—and it rewards his faith and his work with its secrets. So, too, the perplexing mysteries of our human lot remain largely meaningless until we bring to them a faith in the heavenly Father's will. Then the ventures of life make sense where they didn't before. We see areas of meaning and truth where all was confusion before. What we see reflects the faith by which we organize our experience. In asking us, "What do you see?" God asks us to open before him and before ourselves the very center of our lives.

What Do You See?

In his "Vision of the Last Judgment" the English poet William Blake wrote " 'What,' it will be Question'd, 'When the Sun rises, do you not see a round disk of fire somewhat like a Guinea?' O no, no, I see an Innumerable company of the Heavenly host crying, 'Holy, Holy, Holy is the Lord God Almighty!' " Which makes clearer what Jesus could have meant when he said "Blessed are the pure in heart, for they shall see God."

CHAPTER 5

How Can I Give You Up?

*How can I give you up, O Ephraim! How can
I hand you over, O Israel! How can I make
you like Admah! How can I treat you like
Zeboiim! My heart recoils within me, my compassion grows warm and tender. I will not
execute my fierce anger, I will not again destroy Ephraim; for I am God and not man.*
(Hos. 11:8-9)

We hate to hear of a
broken home. Whenever we hear of one it makes our hearts
heavy. For we know that it means that persons have sus-
tained defeat. We know that a man and a woman have
suffered. And if there are children involved, we know not
only that they have suffered, innocently, but that they have
been given a handicap in the venture of life. All this is bad
news.

But from one such tragedy, good news has come. Out of
the darkness of one couple's miserable marriage has come
a word of hope for all other couples of the world, and for
single people as well. These two were not people we know

52

personally, and we did not read of their mishaps in the columns of our daily newspapers. They lived in Palestine —probably in the city of Samaria—some time around 740 years before the birth of Christ. The man was Hosea, son of Beeri, and Gomer, daughter of Diblaim—not that in-laws had anything to do with their troubles. They had three children: two boys and a girl.

Hosea was a prophet. Like Amos, he was one of those strange figures who found himself constrained to speak for God. Like Amos, he looked upon life around him with observant eyes, emotional sensitivity, and a keen conscience. He too was steeped in the rigorous moral tradition that had come down from Moses and Mt. Sinai. To him Israel's covenant relationship with her Lord was the most important thing in the public and private life of her people. It was what made Israel Israel. Hence it was meant to be the basis of all her policies as a nation. Furthermore it was the moral framework within which all her citizens were called to live. This is the heart of all the prophets' word to Israel. This is the concern and constraint shared by them all.

Amos, who was Hosea's contemporary from the southern portion of the divided kingdom, addressed himself mostly to controversial social issues. He scored the great inequality of wealth. He spelled out in dramatic images the corruption of the courts, and of government, by men of great wealth so that the poor man couldn't even keep the little that was his. The trouble with your religion, Amos thundered at the people, is that your morals are bad. They make of your religion a hollow mockery. Hosea was sensitive to social injustice too, but he took hold of the problem at the other end. Whereas Amos said, in effect, "the trouble with your religion is that your morals are bad," Hosea said, in effect, "the trouble with your morals is that your religion is bad." The evils which were so painfully evident in Israel's public affairs were seen by Hosea to be coming from the people's deep alienation from God. Israel was estranged from God, her maker, protector, and hope.

So far as we know, Amos was a bachelor. He went about his prophetic work unhindered by family cares, and uninhibited by family responsibilities. Hosea on the other hand was not only married, and a family man, but he had grave domestic trouble. Not only did this affect the style in which he shaped his message, it opened his eyes to depths in the Eternal and his relationship to men which no one had seen before. And it opened the ears of his heart to a cry from the heart of God that was not anger but anguish.

The awful truth was that Gomer, Hosea's wife, was unfaithful to him—repeatedly so, shamelessly so, to the point of promiscuity. Hosea did not know that the children were his. After years of this humiliating relationship during which Gomer repeatedly disappointed Hosea's hopes, they separated. Knowing this helps us to understand the form which Hosea's message took as he spoke of Israel's relationship to her God. He saw that the covenant between God and Israel was very much like a marriage, and Israel had been faithless in it.

Hear the word of the Lord, O people of Israel;
for the Lord has a controversy with the inhabitants of the land.

There is no faithfulness or kindness,
   and no knowledge of God in the land;
there is swearing, lying, killing, stealing, and committing
     adultery;
   they break all bounds and murder follows murder. (4:1-2)
Wine and new wine
   take away the understanding.
My people inquire of a thing of wood,
   and their staff gives them oracles.
For a spirit of harlotry has led them astray,
   and they have left their God to play the harlot. (4:11-12)

Of what did their infidelity consist? One thing which
Hosea protested was that they worshiped the Eternal God
as though he were a Canaanite fertility idol. The people
addressed God as "my baal." Worse yet, they cast images of
God in the form of a bull, and worshiped them. "That
thing," Hosea shrieked, "a mechanic made it. That is no
God." (See 8:6) "Men kissing calves," he snorted con-
temptuously. (13:2) Here, reasoned Hosea, is the reason
that the fabric of morality is falling to pieces. People cannot
rise far above their religious concepts. What could be expected of a people who worshiped the Eternal God as
though he were a fertility idol whose sole function was to
insure a good harvest and increase the flocks and herds?
When religion is corrupt, behavior will be corrupt.

Thomas Mann gave expression to this fact in a conversa-
tion which he devised between young Joseph in Egypt and
the youthful Pharaoh Ikhnaton (Amenhotep IV) who
was himself a religious man and, like the Hebrews, a be-
liever in one God. "Let me tell you," said Ikhnaton, "men

are a hopeless lot. They know how to do nothing that comes from within themselves, not even the very least thing occurs to them on their own account. They only imitate the gods, and *whatever picture they make of them, that they copy.* Purify the godhead and you purify men." [1] That is precisely what Hosea sought to do—call men back to the purer vision of God which was their heritage.

Israel's harlotry, furthermore, consisted in a naïve reliance upon her kings, according to Hosea. The government of the nation in this period was almost as unstable and ineffective as the fourth republic in France. In the twenty-one years from the death of the strong king, Jeroboam II, until the destruction of Israel by Assyria there were six kings. Some ruled only a month or two. All were overthrown in revolution and murder. Yet each king had his devotees and partisans. The people hoped that this time all would be well, but they never faced the basic religious and moral issues.

> They made kings, but not through me.
> > They set up princes, but without my knowledge
> > > [saith the Lord]. (8:4)
> All their princes are rebels. (9:15)
> For now they will say:
> > "We have no king,
> for we fear not the Lord,
> > and a king, what could he do for us?"
> They [the kings] utter mere words;

[1] *Joseph the Provider,* tr. H. T. Lowe-Porter (New York: Alfred A. Knopf, 1944), p. 194.

56

with empty oaths they make covenants;
so judgment springs up like poisonous weeds
in the furrows of the field. (10:3-4)

Then too, Israel busied herself with military alliances. Assyria was the military power of the day, and was to destroy Israel completely in a few years. So Israel made alliance with Egypt. The rival kings of Israel even made Assyrian alliances against each other. Of this folly Hosea cried:

Ephraim [Israel] mixes himself with the peoples. (7:8)
Aliens devour his strength, and he knows it not. (7:9)
    yet they do not return to the Lord their God,
    nor seek him, for all this. (7:10)
Ephraim is like a dove,
    silly and without sense,
    calling to Egypt, going to Assyria. (7:11)
They do not cry unto me from the heart [saith the
    Lord]. (7:14)

"For they sow the wind, and they shall reap the whirlwind," said Hosea in a phrase that has persisted to this day. (8:7) The prophet concluded that the Lord was ready to wash his hands of Israel as he, Hosea, had washed his hands of Gomer.

But there was the hitch. Hosea hadn't washed his hands of Gomer. He could have had her stoned to death. But he didn't. He still loved her. Despite the violent outrage she had inflicted upon his love—and the degradation she had brought upon herself in so doing—Hosea still loved her.

He thought of her in anger and sorrow, to be sure, but also in tenderness and affection. And despite it all he intended to take her back unto himself as his wife.

It was here in the mysterious grandeur of his own very human love for a woman that Hosea was able to catch a glimpse of the real depths of the Divine Love for his people. In his own anguish over a faithless wife the prophet was able to fathom God's anguish over a faithless people. And the heartsick prophet heard, if not an inquiry, certainly a tortured outcry from the heart of God: "How can I give you up, O Ephraim! How can I hand you over, O Israel!" And through his own dogged intent to redeem his broken home, Hosea saw the persevering grace of God seeking to redeem his broken world. "My heart recoils within me, my compassion grows warm and tender. I will not execute my fierce anger." In his own hope that this time it would be different, Hosea was able to express for a hopeless world its Maker's persisting intent that it shall be as he intended from the beginning.

Therefore I am going to persuade her,
And lead her to the wilderness,
And speak to her heart.

. . . .

And she shall respond there as in the day of her youth,
As in the day when she came up from the land of Egypt.
On that day it shall come to pass, is the oracle of the Lord,
That you will call me, "My husband,"
And you will no longer call me, "My Baal."

. . . .

And I will betroth you to myself forever;

58

I will betroth you to myself in righteousness and justice,
And in kindness and mercy.
And I will betroth you to myself in faithfulness;
And you shall know the Lord.
It shall come to pass on that day, is the oracle of the Lord,
That I will answer the heavens, and they shall answer the
    earth;
And the earth shall answer the grain, the wine, and the oil;
    (2:14-22 Goodspeed)

And the prophet continued, speaking for God through himself:

> What more has Ephraim any need of idols?
> . . . .
> From me is his fruit found. (14:8 Goodspeed)

Through one man's broken home, God's love for sinning humanity was proclaimed. What one man would do to reunite his family, God will do to save his people, was the burden of Hosea's message.

This insight, which was new when Hosea announced it, is a commonplace with us. We speak glibly of God's forgiveness. Indeed, there were some in Hosea's day who took the word lightly:

> Come, let us return to the Lord;
> For he has torn, but he will heal us;
> He smote, but he will bind us up;
> He will revive us in two or three days;
>
> . . . .
> As soon as we seek him, we shall find him;

> He will come to us like . . . the spring rain that
> waters the land. (6:1-3 Goodspeed)

Before Hosea had finished proclaiming the forgiveness of God, people were taking it for granted, and people have been taking it for granted ever since.

"How can I give you up!" God's forgiveness is there—as high as human arrogance, as wide as human sin, as deep as human degradation. That is the gospel. That is the good news. But let us never think of it as cheap or easy. The image of it is not that of a multimillionaire imperiously waving on an urchin who has thrown a baseball through a small window. Its image is not that of a senile grandfather laughing off the rudeness of his grandchildren whom he can't manage anyhow. Nor is its image that of an overindulgent parent too softhearted to prevent Junior from becoming a little monster. These are not the images of God's mercy and forgiveness.

The image of it is rather that of a heartsick husband rising above his humiliation to take to his breast hopefully once more a promiscuous wife and her children whom he had never ceased to love. More clearly yet we see it in the Divine Love, incarnate, draped in human spittle and wearing a crown of thorns. "How can I give you up!" God's forgiveness is good news. But let us never forget its cost. Its symbols are a prophet's broken home and a Savior's broken body.

CHAPTER 6

What Are You Doing Here?

And there he came to a cave, and lodged there;
and behold, the word of the Lord came to
him, and he said to him, "What are you doing
here, Elijah?" He said, "I have been very
jealous for the Lord, the God of hosts; for the
people of Israel have forsaken thy covenant,
thrown down thy altars, and slain thy prophets
with the sword; and I, even I only, am left;
and they seek my life, to take it away."

(I Kings 19:9-10)

The career of the proph-
et Elijah was earlier than those of Amos and Hosea by more
than a hundred years. He lived in a day when Hebrew
religion was still primitive and crude. Yet crude as it was
it was incomparably superior, intellectually and morally,
to the fertility religion of the Canaanites among whom the
Hebrews had taken residence. One may justifiably conclude
that God was disclosing himself, as rapidly and as fully
as they could bear it, through the Hebrew people to all
mankind. The prophets of Israel of which Elijah was an

early representative, to be followed in God's good time by the more religiously refined Amos, Isaiah, and Hosea, were bearers of God's self-disclosure and spokesmen of it. It was through them that Israel was brought new light as the time demanded, and as she was ready for it. And it was through them that Israel was called back, from time to time, to the light she had already attained, but lost.

Elijah is best remembered for his bitter conflict with King Ahab of Israel. Ahab came to the throne of Israel around 875 B.C. And, according to scripture, "Ahab . . . did evil in the sight of the Lord more than all that were before him" (I Kings 16:30). Ahab's chief trouble appears to be that he was henpecked. His wife, the former Sidonian princess Jezebel, was a formidable hussy whose name has become a common noun in our language. Jezebel was a hearty and evangelistic devotee of Baal, the fertility god. She not only converted her husband, but sought to convert all Israel and undertook to stamp out the worship of the Lord. She almost did it too. A temple to Baal was erected in the city of Samaria, and at the queen's behest the Hebrew prophets were killed or driven underground.

Into this fray Elijah entered at grave personal danger. The story as preserved for us in the book of Kings is that Elijah arranged a showdown. (I Kings 18:17 ff.) He dared Ahab to assemble the people at Mt. Carmel. There the prophet, in the name of the God of Israel, would challenge 450 priests of the pagan religion. Ahab accepted the dare, and the people assembled. Elijah scored the people about their vacillation and indecision—"limping with two different opinions"—and then demanded that they make up their minds once and for all. "If the Lord is God, follow him; but if Baal, then follow him." There had never been room in the religion of Israel for a comfortable blending of faiths, for the word of the Lord through Moses was that they should have no other gods besides him.

Elijah then arranged a test which was as exclusive as such a rigorous religion demanded, and which appealed as being fair to the devotees of both sides. He arranged for two fires to be laid but not lit. Upon each pile of wood a sacrificed bull was to be cut up and laid. The priests of Baal were to appeal to their god to consume the offering with fire, and Elijah was to do the same. Whichever god answered in such a manner was manifestly the real God. This plan was followed. The priests of Baal prepared their sacrificial pyre and danced about it in their manner, crying aloud and lacerating their flesh for the better part of the day. Nothing happened. Elijah couldn't resist this opportunity to poke a little fun at his rivals. He suggested to them that they yell a little louder, for perhaps their deity was asleep, or was lost in his own thoughts, or was away on business, or perhaps in the celestial equivalent of the bathroom.[1] When the priests of Baal were exhausted, Elijah called the people to him while he calmly and symbolically repaired a destroyed altar to the Lord, and prepared upon it his sacrifice. Furthermore he doused it with twelve jars of water, not so much, it is thought, to make the test harder, but to suggest an ending of the three-year drought that had brought affairs to this crisis between the two religions.

[1] See commentaries on I Kings 18:27.

Then, in marked contrast to the frenzy of the priests of Baal, the prophet approached his God in the dignity of prayer: "O Lord, God of Abraham, Isaac, and Israel, let it be known this day that thou art God in Israel, and that I am thy servant, and that I have done all these things at thy word. Answer me, O Lord, answer me, that this people may know that thou, O Lord, art God, and that thou hast turned their hearts back." The fire came, and consumed the offering. Some students of the Bible have suggested that, since oilfields are now known to be in that area, the water which Elijah used had a high naphtha content. Others think that at just that moment lightning hit the heaped up altar. In any event, the people were convinced. Then Elijah, having yet to learn the mercy of God which Hosea was to declare more than a century later, turned the wrath of the mob on the prophets of Baal, and had all of them killed at Kishon Brook. He then told Ahab that although there had been three years of drought, and although the only cloud in sight was no bigger than a man's hand, Ahab had better drive his chariot home quickly before he got stuck in the mud. Then in sheer exhilaration at the decisive and dramatic victory of his faith, he raced the chariot on foot as the rains came.

Jezebel was not pleased. She gave Elijah just twenty-four hours to live. Perhaps it was an emotional letdown, a psychological backlash, but Elijah became afraid. This rugged old prophet who had dared so much, and fought so courageously, and stood so firm, went to pieces. Here was his enemy bouncing back with a vengeance. His "decisive" victory was proving to be far from decisive. Indeed, the fight of high religion against lower forms of religion is never completely finished. It has to be continued from age to age, including our own. But Elijah had had enough. He could go no further. He couldn't take it any more. He fled into the desert and found the paltry shade of a broom tree. There he asked the Lord that he might die, for his efforts had done no good. "I've had it," he said in effect. "It is enough; now, O Lord, take away my life; for I am no better than my fathers." Then in utter physical and emotional exhaustion he fell asleep.

Now that is all right. We can feel deeply for a fatigued old man whose enemies bid fair to outlast him despite his supreme effort. Elijah was certainly entitled to a vacation, not to mention a good sleep. In fact, he was about due to retire. But Elijah was quitting—running away. When he awoke rested, he did not return to the fray in Samaria. He kept going southward toward Mt. Sinai. When he got there, he found himself a cave, and lodged there. As far as Elijah was concerned, he was through.

One day, however, when Elijah was out on a mountain ridge, a mighty storm burst upon it. The wind screamed among the crags and sent loose boulders toppling. The whole mountain seemed to shake with the fury of it. Perhaps there were some avalanches, minor earthquakes, or some volcanic rumbling. And there was fire from heaven—lightning—hitting a pinnacle or blasting a tree and leaving it burning. Here was all the power of nature displayed spectacularly about this awesome and hallowed mountain where Moses had received the law of the Lord centuries before. Elijah was awed as had been the children of Israel

65

by the storms about the head of Mt. Sinai which was thought to be singularly the dwelling place of the Lord.

Elijah realized that the storm was not the Lord. But in the silence that followed the storm, made doubly still by contrast, the tired old prophet heard the voice within which *was* the voice of God. And it asked, "What are you doing here, Elijah?" What are you doing *here*—in hiding, miles from the scene of your work? Elijah whimpered his reply: "I have been very jealous for the Lord, the God of hosts; for the people of Israel have forsaken thy covenant, thrown down thy altars, and slain thy prophets with the sword; and I even I only am left; and they seek my life, to take it away." God's reply through the voice of a conscience that had long been attuned to divine imperatives was this: Go back. You shall yet live to anoint a new king over Syria, and another king over Israel. And you shall live to inaugurate your successor. Oh, and Elijah—there are seven thousand Israelites besides yourself who have not bowed to Baal.

Here was Elijah, huddling in the cave of fear. "They seek my life to take it away." In this case it was true, and that would frighten most people. But how many of us take to the caves of fear on so much lesser provocation. How many of us are immobilized by fears that have so little grounds, or fears of such little things. We fear criticism—that others will speak unkindly of us. We fear ridicule—that others will laugh at our efforts or simply consider us naïve or quixotic. We fear failure—that we will stand condemned by our own consciences or fall short of our own expectations for ourselves. We fear rejection—that those whose approval we need will rebuff us or refuse the "forlorn, confiding gestures" of our hearts. Here we cower in the caves of fear—fear of fates not half so bad, really, as genuinely hostile persecution, much less death. And God's inquiry to us, as to Elijah, is "What are you doing here? Do you doubt that I am able to care for my own? Have you forgotten the providence that has brought you this far upon your way? Do you think I have forgotten you? Where is that touch of holy recklessness which is the surest mark of faith?" Carol Wise has observed that the man of mature faith is able to accept either life or death because he has lost his fear of both.[2] And Donald Hankey, according to Leslie Weatherhead, used to lead his men against the enemy in the first world war, saying, "Come on, men! If you're hit, it's Blighty. If you're killed, it's the resurrection."[3] What are we doing here in the cave of fear?

Furthermore, Elijah was lodged in a crevice of self-pity. Put together his statement that his enemies were out to get him, and his statement that he had been very zealous for the Lord, and a rather clear picture of the prophet's inner predicament emerges. After an exciting and rewarding life in the service of the Most High, Elijah had begun to feel sorry for himself. He had begun to feel that life had given him something less than fair treatment, and that he deserved something better. And he was brooding upon it, and pouting.

We get stuck in that crevice too; and what a death trap of the spirit it is! I do believe that it is the deadliest of all

[2] *Psychiatry and the Bible* (New York: Harper and Bros., 1956), p. 65.
[3] *Prescription for Anxiety* (Nashville: Abingdon Press, 1956), p. 86.

attitudes to take possession of a human mind. Everyone suffers reverses and misfortunes of some kind during his lifetime. Sometimes these things come at the hands of men, as in Elijah's case, and sometimes they are the freaks of fate. But we are built with considerable resiliency in us. A person can bounce back from most adversity, and still live a life that is to some degree useful and satisfying to both himself and others. The idea surely crosses the mind of every person at some time or other that his difficulties are more than average, and that he has had a dirty deal, and that men and the world generally are against him. If he lets that idea grow and take possession of him, he is done for. It is the devil's most effective weapon for destroying the will and all that is healthy and sound and creative in the human mind. A person who wallows in self-pity *is* through. John Sutherland Bonnell told of a New York minister who visited Sing Sing penitentiary, and with the warden's permission interviewed nineteen of the prisoners there. One question he asked each prisoner in turn was "Why are you here?" Some of the answers he received were these: "I was framed. They ganged up on me." "Well, the police have had it in for me since I was a kid and they had their chance and vented a grudge on me." Some variation on this theme was voiced by every one of the nineteen prisoners. The minister said later that he had never come across so many completely innocent people in one place.[4] That attitude is probably the largest single factor in explaining the presence of them all at Sing Sing.

[4] *The Pulpit,* August, 1956.

No wonder that God asks us relentlessly, continually, "What are you doing here? Have you forgotten all that has made your life worth the living, and still makes it so? Have you forgotten your moments of victory? Have you lost your perspective completely? Do you no longer notice the loads that others carry, and the reverses they sustain? Will you really surrender all your talent, all your privileges, and all your potential to that one filthy obsession?"

Ned Roberts is a missionary at Mondombe in the Belgian Congo. He tells that one day he was looking over his wash-bowl that had been broken, and was feeling rather sorry for himself amid the austerities and inconveniences of missionary life, when he heard a cough outside the door. He opened the door to find a Congolese minister-teacher standing there with a note from Dr. Donald Baker, the station physician. It read, "I find this evangelist to be a leper. He wants to go into the leper colony. Sorry. Don." Roberts, severely jolted, began to offer his sympathy to his African colleague, but the man replied that he was not surprised at the diagnosis. There had been considerable leprosy in his family. Now that he had it, he wanted an assignment to continue his Christian work among other victims of the disease. Arrangements were made for him to serve as minister-teacher in the leper colony. Roberts sheepishly eyed his broken wash bowl, got some pliers and a piece of wire and bound the bowl together so that it would hold water. Every time he uses the leaky bowl, or begins to feel sorry for himself, the missionary relates, he is reminded of the leper, and how the power of faith in Christ makes men serviceable for him. What are we doing here, you and I, lodged in the crevice of self-pity?

Nor were these the only developments in the life of his prophet Elijah that led God to accost him with a searching inquiry. Elijah was also posturing on the peak of self-righteousness. "The people of Israel have forsaken thy covenant, thrown down thy altars, slain thy prophets—and I, even I only, am left." There was some truth, God knows, in what Elijah had said. But the world wasn't as bad, nor he as virtuous, as he supposed. This Elijah complex is a besetting sin of good and respectable people—and of religious people in particular. I have heard honest workingmen imply that they are the only union men left who give a day's work for a day's wages. I have heard parents claim to be the only ones left who try to teach their children manners. I have heard cultivated people insinuate that they are among the very very few remaining in America who aren't outright Philistines. And of course, many are the devoted church folks who fancy themselves to be the only ones concerned with the declining level of modern morals. "I, even I only, am left."

"You are presumptuous aren't you, little man" is the inquiry of our God when he manages to get through to us in our mountain fastness. "Do you really think that you are the only one who cares? Do you really fancy that no others respond any more to my workings within their hearts? Do you honestly believe that my Spirit is unable to inspire any others to constancy and valor as I have inspired you? Do you dare to overlook your predecessors in the faith and your co-workers of today, and your successors to come, in

70

fighting a good fight at whatever posts they find themselves? Now go back and join the seven thousand others who have not bowed at pagan altars, and finish your work, and cast your mantle gracefully upon the shoulders of your successor."

Or as an early Christian wrote to his beleaguered comrades: "Therefore, since we are surrounded by so great a cloud of witnesses, let us also lay aside every weight, and sin which clings so closely, and let us run with perseverance the race that is set before us, looking to Jesus the pioneer and perfecter of our faith, who for the joy that was set before him endured the cross, despising the shame, and is seated at the right hand of the throne of God." (Heb. 12:1-2.)

CHAPTER 7

Should Not I Pity Nineveh?

And the Lord said, "You pity the plant, for which you did not labor, nor did you make it grow, which came into being in a night, and perished in a night. And should not I pity Nineveh, that great city, in which there are more than a hundred and twenty thousand persons who do not know their right hand from their left, and also much cattle?"

(Jonah 4:10-11)

The book of Jonah is a parable. It is neither history nor biography. It is a parable —a story told for teaching purposes. We are familiar with such vivid teaching devices, for they were copiously used by our Lord. The best-known ones are his stories of the good Samaritan and the prodigal son. Whether or not these figures were actual men who lived at a given time and place probably never entered Jesus' mind, nor the minds of his hearers, nor ours. So it is with the parable of Jonah. We may happily forget the formidable technical difficulties which Jonah would have encountered during

72

three days in the interior of a huge fish. And we may properly occupy our minds rather with what the writer of the
story was driving at. What is the point of the parable?

The book of Jonah has rightly been placed among the
books of prophecy in the Bible. It is in the best tradition of
Jewish prophecy. But the prophet, of course, is *not* Jonah
the son of Amittai. The *author of the story* is the prophet.
We honor not Hamlet, Prince of Denmark; we honor William Shakespeare. And just as the story of Hamlet tells us
that Shakespeare knew human emotion, the story of Jonah
tells us that its author was a man sensitive to the will and
the ways of God. This author, whoever he was, lived some-
time between 400 B.C. and 200 B.C. This was long after the
Israel to whom Elijah and Amos and Hosea spoke had
been destroyed by Assyria in 721 B.C. It was also long after
the Judah to whom Isaiah spoke had been carried off by
the Babylonians. The Judeans had been taken captive by
Babylon in 582 B.C., and had returned to their homeland
in 538 B.C.

The period following their return from Babylonian exile
was a period of intense nationalism and isolationism among
the Jewish people. But for that matter, what period isn't?
And what people are devoid of this spirit? What sentiment
is more common, around the world and through the ages,
than patriotism? The only exceptions I know are the frosty
citizens of Lower Slobbovia, and that is what makes Al
Capp's fictional country so funny. What feelings are more
easily aroused, around the world in any century, than suspicion and dislike of foreigners and all things foreign?
Nationalism (or Arnold Toynbee's more inclusive and ac-

curate term, parochialism) is the most common of outlooks. In some times and places it is mild; in other times and places it is virulent. In some times and places it is relatively enlightened; in other times and places it is entirely bigoted. In Judah after the people had returned from exile in Babylon, nationalism was virulent and bigoted. Under the leadership of Ezra, the priest, religion and narrow patriotism reinforced each other. In fact they became virtually one and the same thing. Nothing makes a nation quite so intolerant—and intolerable. It was into this kind of situation that our unknown prophet introduced his parable, or allegory, of Jonah.

The figure of Jonah, as the Jewish people who heard the story realized—to their discomfort—represented *them.* He was a symbol of the Jewish people—of Judah. And God had given him a job to do. He was to go to Nineveh, "that great city," as a spokesman for God. Nineveh had been the capital of the ancient Assyrian empire. In this story it is a symbol for the whole wicked hostile gentile world. Jonah was called upon to teach Nineveh, and to bring it into a saving relationship to the Lord. Jonah did not relish that task. When God told him to go east to Nineveh he booked passage instead on a ship that was going west to Spain.

It is Jonah's adventures at sea that have become the most familiar part of his story, unfortunately. The Lord sent a great storm upon the ship. Jonah discerned the meaning of the storm because his own conscience convicted him. He told the sailors that he was to blame for the plight of them all. The heathen sailors are pictured by the author as being ignorant and superstitious, but nevertheless basically decent fellows. They did all that they could to save the ship before they resorted to the penitent Jonah's unselfish suggestion that they cast him into the raging billows. But when their sturdiest efforts availed nothing the sailors decided that the guilty man must be sacrificed. And Jonah went into the drink. Thereupon Jonah was swallowed whole, conscience and all, by a huge fish which the Lord had sent by for that purpose. And therein, despite the poor ventilation, Jonah meditated upon his responsibilities and the dismal consequences of his having avoided them. After this, the fish spit him out upon his native shore. The Jewish people would have had little difficulty in recognizing the whole of Jonah's episode with the fish as representing their own captivity in Babylon, and their recent return to their homeland.

Again Jonah was reminded of his job. And this time Jonah went to Nineveh—not, however, with great enthusiasm. If he couldn't avoid foreigners altogether, the next best thing, he thought, was to deliver the Lord's ultimatum as quickly and as unpleasantly as possible. They won't accept of course, thought Jonah, and so I will hurry back out of the city and watch the consequences. It was in this redemptive spirit that God's reluctant representative plodded sullenly into the city of Nineveh to go through the motions of his mission. Then he hastily withdrew to what he fancied was a safe distance, built himself a little shelter, and began a count-down. The author's portrayal here of his people's frame of mind toward their divine mission has the bite of fine satire. The figure of Jonah represents to perfection the Jews' distaste for any contaminating

contact with foreigners, the formal and external nature of
their obedience to the divine commission, and their essen-
tial lovelessness in this period of their national history.
Jonah in his pathetic little shelter, hoping for the worst
for the rest of the world, was an image of themselves
equally difficult for the Jews to misinterpret or to swallow.

To Jonah's horror, in place of fire from heaven destroying
an unrepentant city, mercy from heaven forgave a re-
pentant one. In the parable, Nineveh actually responded to
the divine word which Jonah had so gracelessly borne. This
made Jonah mad enough to die, and he told the Lord so.
So the Lord in turn was obliged to teach Jonah another
little lesson. The story continues with God causing a plant
to grow up to shade Jonah where he sat pouting. Jonah was
exceedingly pleased with the shade, even though its source
was a lowly castor oil plant. The next day, the story continues, God sent a worm to kill the plant, and Jonah was
in a state nearing apoplexy. Then God drove home a truth
into the cramped and parochial mind of his reluctant little
servant. "You pity the plant, for which you did not labor,
nor did you make it grow, which came into being in a
night, and perished in a night. And *should not I pity
Nineveh*, that great city, in which there are more than a
hundred and twenty thousand persons who do not know
their right hand from their left, and also much cattle?"

"Should not I pity Nineveh?" What a load that inquiry
of God carried to the unknown prophet who heard it and
set it down in the parable of Jonah. What a load it carried
to the people of Judah in the days of Ezra the priest, who
heard this parable and got the point. And what a jolt this

authentic inquiry of God carries to us American Christians
—particularly to any of us who regularly spend more on
dog food than we give to the world mission enterprise of
the Church.

It implies, for instance, that we have a responsibility to
Nineveh. Israel's special place in God's economy was not
merely something to be gloried in and enjoyed. It was first
and foremost a mission to the world. The prophets all called
their people back to this mission every time they forgot it.
If you are going to eat at the training table, you have to
dress for the game. There is no master-race complex involved in having a sense of America's mission to the world.
A decent sense of stewardship and fair play gives the same
answer. We are too well fed, too comfortable, too wealthy,
too fortunate not to have some special role in the divine
economy. Henry Smith Leiper, for illustrative purposes,
metaphorically compressed the 2,500,000,000 people in
the world into a town of one thousand inhabitants. On
this scale, sixty of the villagers would be Americans and 940
would be all the other peoples of the world. These sixty
villagers would have one half of the total income in the
town. And despite the fact that they would eat 72 per cent
more than is good for them, these sixty would have a life
expectancy of seventy years against an expectancy of forty
years for the average among the 940 other residents who,
for the most part, would be poor, hungry, sick, and ignorant.
We have a job to do for the human race—a mission to
Nineveh. Even if this truth doesn't get through to us as
Americans, surely it must reach us as Christians. Do we
really believe that Christian teaching lifts human life? Do

we really believe that it liberates the mind, spurs the will, kindles imagination, and warms the affections? Do we believe that only Christian premises support political liberty, and only Christian conduct makes it work? "The ground is level at the foot of the cross," said Franklin Clark Fry. "I challenge you! Do you know any place else where it is level? Democracy is an empty fiction without the equality resulting from Christ's death for all." Should we not share the Christian faith with as many Ninevites as possible, and Americans as well?

Another implication of the divine inquiry is that Nineveh is persons. "Should not I pity Nineveh, that great city, in which there are more than a hundred and twenty thousand *persons?*" To Jonah and the people of Judah, Nineveh was merely the hostile capital of heathendom. But the heavenly Father saw it as he sees all the cities of the world—as the homes of men, women, and children, his children all. Nineveh is persons. Hiroshima is persons. Nagasaki is persons. London is persons. Berlin is persons. Cairo, Moscow, Peking, Washington, and Wichita—all are the homes of God's children. How we need the divine perspective as we go about preparing and testing bombs that will obliterate the largest city in one flash, and as we go about preparing rockets to deliver them by night.

The intolerable absurdity of preparations for war in this day and age was unintentionally dramatized by an article in a recent popular magazine showing how citizens might survive in the event of nuclear war by making use of prefabricated bomb shelters to be buried in back yards. These shelters had two entrances—one into the cellar of the house and one into the outdoors—"in accord with the ingenious plan devised a million years ago by rabbits," observed Roland Bainton of Yale, who then went on to muse that the denizens of these dugouts will be able to pray:

> God of the rabbit and the mole,
> We thank thee for our plastic hole,
> Where, refugees from cosmic rays,
> We spend congested holidays.
> When blooms the crocus, buoyed with hope
> We view it through a periscope.[1]

I presume that the plans in Moscow to protect its citizens from atomization are equally ludicrous. One would think that if the common sense of the world's peoples would not force their leaders to negotiate, and negotiate, and negotiate, and negotiate, their sense of the ridiculous would.

Nineveh is persons. That is the tragedy of the present condition of our world. But that is also our hope. T. S. Eliot in the second world war rightly saw that our only alternatives are the holocaust of war or the refining fire of a conversion of mind. Referring to the dive bombers, he wrote:

> The dove descending breaks the air
> With flame of incandescent terror
> Of which the tongues declare
> The one discharge from sin and error.
> The only hope, or else despair
>   Lies in the choice of pyre or pyre—
>   To be redeemed from fire by fire.

[1] "Christian Pacifism Reassessed," *The Christian Century*, July 23, 1958.

> Who then devised the torment? Love.
> Love is the unfamiliar Name
> Behind the hands that wove
> The intolerable shirt of flame
> Which human power cannot remove.
>   We only live, only suspire
>   Consumed by either fire or fire.[2]

God's inquiry "Should not I pity Nineveh?" carries the hopeful implication that even Ninevites can undergo a transformation under divine influences, however haltingly expressed by men. Since Nineveh is persons, Nineveh can repent.

God's inquiry carries the further implication that the judgment of Nineveh is God's to make—not Jonah's. God wasn't concerned that Nineveh become like Jerusalem. He wanted its citizens to repent. Yes. (He wanted Jerusalem to repent, for that matter.) But in the story he was satisfied, for the time at least, that Nineveh respond to his overtures after its own genius—not that it become another Jerusalem. Now that is an insight that Jonah never achieved, and we have trouble with it too. As Christians our mission is to take Christ, however imperfect our understanding of him, to pagan cultures for them to respond to his love in their own way. Our job is not to make Asians and Africans, much less the Kremlin or Peking, into our image. Insofar as Christian missions have taken Christ to persons of the Orient and Africa, they have borne fruit acceptable to God

[2] From "Little Gidding" in *Four Quartets* by T. S. Eliot, copyright, 1943, by T. S. Eliot. Reprinted by permission of Harcourt, Brace and Company, Inc.

and benign to men. And they will continue to do so in ways we cannot now foresee. Insofar as Christian missions have sought to be a transplanting of Western manners and outlooks, they have backfired in our faces. Unfortunately in this heated hour of world-wide revolution, neither we nor they have always been able to make this all-important distinction.

It was not long ago that the Dutch were ejected forcibly from Indonesia. Now the Dutch can probably claim to be as Christian as any modern nation, and Dutch churches have spent money on Christian missions. Nevertheless, Indonesian Christians participated in the revolution that took their country out from under Dutch control. At the time when the conflict and tension were near their height, the Indonesian Council of Churches addressed a circular letter to their Dutch colleagues expressing regret for the excesses visited upon them. Then they added:

We hope that you will continue to perform your duties and fulfill your professional responsibilities. . . . We will do everything in our power to sustain you and make it possible for you to carry on the work to which you were called when you were invited to Indonesia. Our prayers go out to you and to your families.

Another statement added:

We cannot anticipate even the events of tomorrow. . . . Nevertheless as Christians we are confident that, as the socio-economic revolution works itself out, God is in the process, and that all things will work together for good to those who love the Lord. Ours is a faith which accepts tragedy as the inevitable concomitant of history, but which transcends tragedy through faith in the resurrected Lord.[3]

Asian Christians will still be Asians; European Christians will still be Europeans; American Christians will still be Americans. But the judgment of all belongs to God, not to each other. For as John Saltmarsh observed so truly—"My truth is as dark to thee as thy truth is dark to me until the Lord enlighten all our seeing."

[3] Winburn T. Thomas, "Testing Time in Indonesia," *The Christian Century,* Jan. 22, 1958.

CHAPTER 8

Shall a Faultfinder Contend with the Almighty?

Then the Lord answered Job out of the whirl-
wind: Who is this that darkens counsel by
words without knowledge? Gird up your loins
like a man, I will question you, and you shall
declare to me. . . . And the Lord said to Job:
"Shall a faultfinder contend with the Al-
mighty? He who argues with God, let him
answer it." (Job 38:1-3; 40:1-2)

Arguing with God is precisely what Job had been doing. Not actually, of course, because the book of Job is a play, not a biography. Job is therefore a literary figure, not a historical one. But through the words of the figure of Job some ancient author had indeed been arguing with God. He was arguing the problem of evil. By "the problem of evil" religious people mean a very specific thing. It is a singularly perplexing problem for all those who believe not only that God exists, but that he is the creator of the heavens and the earth, and that he is also good. Our unknown author—and hence his spokesman, Job—did believe all these things. The problem of evil, simply stated, is this: *If* the universe is the work of a God who is good, why is there so much evil in it? Why is there so much sin? And why is it that not only do the sinners suffer for their sins, but why also do people who are manifestly good suffer, and why do children who are manifestly innocent suffer as well? Now that is a problem both real and tormenting.

If there be no God then the presence of evil in the world is no problem. It is just the way the atoms bounce. It may be terribly unpleasant, but it raises no questions. It may be a practical problem, but not an intellectual or spiritual one. If there be no God at all, then a person may do whatever he can to avoid cancer or cure it, but if he should contract cancer he would have no reason to cry, "Why did this happen to me?" If there be no God at all, a person may detest war and try to prevent it, but it would not occur to him to ask, "Why does God permit such things?" If innocent children are destroyed by storm or flood—and there be no God—we would say "I'm sorry," but we would not be moved to ask, "How can this be?" The problem of evil simply isn't there as an intellectual or spiritual torment if there be no God.

The same is true if God be evil or capricious. In that case we are his playthings, as some primitive and ancient peoples have believed, and as some disillusioned modern people believe. "As flies to wanton boys, so are we to the gods," cried King Lear in Shakespeare's play. This is extremely unpleasant if it be true. But it is not the problem of evil as

Job faced it. The problem disappears too if God be something less than the creator of the universe. Some thinkers, for instance, believe God to be a figure of speech, or another name for our human ideals and conscience, or a personification of the good, the true, and the beautiful—nice but rather ineffectual. God, so conceived, does not make the presence of evil in the world a baffling mystery, nor the suffering of the innocent a spiritual problem.

But God is. He is good. He is a person, not a personification. He is the ultimate source of the worlds and all that is in them. And so the presence of sin, and of human suffering—particularly if undeserved—is a vexing mystery. I have observed that when college students voice their deepest doubts about religion it is usually some restatement of this ancient problem. I have heard it stated too in teen-age slang by youngsters who had no awareness that their own misgivings were those of religious people throughout the centuries. Mature minds, too, grapple with it today. Archibald Macleish's magnificent play, *J.B.*, borrows its form as well as its name from the ancient drama of Job in having a fresh go at this classic issue. The late A. Eustace Haydon, who himself did not believe in God, once said in class that this problem of evil was the rock upon which all theism (belief in God) is ultimately wrecked. To Haydon, evil in a world supposed created by a good God was an impossibility and a contradiction. Since evil is so obviously real, God is not, was his viewpoint.

This, then, is the problem with which the author of the book of Job was wrestling. The book begins with a prologue which many scholars think is simply a setting of the stage rather than a serious explanation of the source of man's suffering. In it we are introduced to Job who was a good man, and prosperous as orthodox religion believed good men would inevitably be. And God was proud of him. The Devil said to God that Job ought to be pious, considering the way it had paid off. The Devil then made God something like a wager that if God were to take away Job's prosperity and comfort, Job would curse God to his face. God could not let such a challenge stand, and so he permitted Satan to destroy in crushing succession Job's possessions, his family, and his health. This is the prologue. (Similarly, many scholars feel that a happy-ending epilogue was attached, by the author or someone else, for those who want it.) The main drama consists in a series of dialogues between the miserable Job and three of his friends who came to comfort him, or something, where he sat upon an ash heap. This interchange is the most eloquent and searching exploration of the problem of evil to be found in literature. Job's friends voiced the easy answers of religious orthodoxy in both their valid insights and their inadequacy —that he who suffers is not really innocent, that suffering is good for a man's character, that the injustice of the situation is only temporary. But Job insisted upon more honest assessment of the realities of the situation which demand more profound answers.

Job did not deny God's existence. But he did raise some extremely pointed questions about God's goodness. He implied quite strongly that God is something of a bully.

Behold, he snatches away; who can hinder him? (9:12)
He will not let me get my breath. (9:18)
If it is a contest of strength, behold him!
If it is a matter of justice, who can summon him [to trial]?
(9:19)
He destroys both the blameless and the wicked.

.   .   .   .

He mocks at the calamity of the innocent.

.   .   .   .

If it is not he, who then is it? (9:22 ff.)
Are not the days of my life few? Let me alone that I may
   find a little comfort (10:20)
I will say to God,

.   .   .   .

Does it seem good to thee to oppress,
   to despise the work of thy hands and favor the designs
   of the wicked? (10:2-3)
I would speak to the Almighty, and
I desire to argue my case with God. (13:3)
Behold, he will slay me; I have no hope;
Yet I will defend my ways to his face. (13:15)
Surely now God has worn me out. (16:7)

Through the mouth of Job, our ancient writer seemed
about to "solve" the problem of evil by asserting that God
himself is unfair, mean, and downright cruel. "As flies
to wanton boys, so are we to the gods."

But it is at about this point in its development that the
bearing of the drama changes. Man ceases to question
God, and hears God question him. As our author pushed
his angered queries deeper and deeper into the heavens

87

he felt the patient void stiffen and the questions turn back upon himself.

> And the Lord said to Job: "Shall a faultfinder contend
>   with the Almighty?" (40:2)
> Gird up your loins like a man;
>   *I* will question *you* and you declare to me.
> Will you even put me in the wrong?
> Will you condemn me that you may be justified? (40:7-8)

Then follows a lyrical survey of all the magnificence of the created world through which our author found himself to be questioned and made humble once more. Out of a whirlwind the Lord questioned Job:

> Where were you when I laid the foundation of the earth?
> . . . .
>   When the morning stars sang together . . . ? (38:4-7)
> Who shut in the sea with doors,
> . . . .
>   And said "Here shall your proud waves be stayed"?
>   (38:8-11)
> Have you commanded the morning,
>   and caused the dawn to know its place? (38:12)
> Who has cleft a channel for the torrents of rain,
>   and a way for the thunderbolt? (38:25)
> Can you bind the chains of the Pleiades,
>   or loose the cords of Orion? (38:31)
> Do you know the ordinances of the heavens?
>   Can you establish their rule on the earth? (38:33)
> Who provides for the raven its prey,
>   when its young ones cry to God? (38:41)

Do you know when the mountain goats bring forth?
  Do you observe the calving of the hinds? (39:1)
Do you give the horse his might?
  Do you clothe his neck with strength? (39:19)
Is it by your wisdom that the hawk soars,

. . . .

Is it at your command that the eagle mounts up
  and makes his nest on high? (39:26-27)
Deck yourself with majesty and dignity;

. . . .

Look on every one that is proud, and bring him low;
  and tread down the wicked where they stand.

. . . .

Then will I also acknowledge to you,
  that your own right hand can give you victory. (40:10-14)

Job could not stand up under such considerations. Who
could? But the point of it all was not simply that God
could overwhelm men with majesty and mystery. Job
knew that already, and so do we. At least in part, God's
stately recitations of the wonders of creation were to re-
store to Job his perspective even in the midst of his suffering. In the riddle of his undeserved suffering Job had
forgotten entirely the greater riddle of his previous undeserved happiness. He was looking at the problem from
only one end. The greater wonder is not that there is so
much evil in our world, but that there is so much that is
good. The problem for our understanding is not that there
is so much disorder in the universe, but that there is so
much order. The issue for our spirits is not alone that God

permits so much suffering, but that He has made possible so much delight—so much that is enjoyable, so much that sustains and supports us, so much that is beautiful and clean and holy. The problem of evil is not the rock on which all belief in God must ultimately flounder. The presence of good is the rock upon which all disbelief must flounder.

> Is it not by his high superfluousness we know
> Our God? For to equal a need
> Is natural, animal, mineral: but to fling
> Rainbows over the rain
> And beauty above the moon, and secret rainbows
> On the domes of deep sea-shells,
> And make the necessary embrace of breeding
> Beautiful also as fire,
> Not even the weeds to multiply without blossom
> Nor the birds without music:
> There is the great humaneness at the heart of
>   things,
> The extravagant kindness, the fountain
> Humanity can understand, and would flow likewise
> If power and desire were perch-mates.[1]

And is there not more here too in the Divine recital of the glories of the created world? May we not, in all reverence, detect in God's questioning of Job the quality of a plea—an appeal for human patience and understanding. And more. Omnipotence need not to have stooped to reply to man's fretful complaints; only love needed to do that.

[1] Copyright 1941 by Robinson Jeffers. Reprinted from *Be Angry at the Sun and Other Poems*, by Robinson Jeffers, by permission of Random House, Inc.

Arbitrary power need not to have condescended to answer weakness by drawing back the veil a bit to reveal not only the glory of creatorhood, *but also the awesome responsibilities and the awful weight of it.* Yet this note is present in God's reply to Job, revealing that although God is not answerable to his created beings, neither does he hold them in contempt. Job's complaints were afforded at least the dignity of a reply, not the utter disdain of silence.

A further implication of God's reply—not wholly anticipated by the author of the drama of Job—is that in pointing out how good creation is, the Creator reveals that it is as good as he can make it alone. As modern men may we not infer what was still beyond the ancient's vision—that if life's cruelties are to be tempered to men, men will have to help do it? And if her bounties are to be extended, men will have to help do that too. Conversely, when God taunted Job to bring down the wicked and establish justice on earth by the might of his own arm, did he not point up the fact that many human iniquities are beyond human power to deal with? The next step in meeting the whole complex of suffering and sin is for men and God to come closer together in plan and work.

But this was not all that lay beyond the ken of our author, for all his honesty, his insight, and his basic trust that, despite all, he would live to see God on his side. For the element of chronology plays its part. At the time our author lived God had not yet said his last word upon the problem of evil in his universe. God had not yet made his most costly assault upon the powers of darkness and sin. He had not yet made his most sacrificial demonstration of his care for men—indeed, of his oneness with them—in their suffering and pain. Still in the future was his most exquisite appeal to the hearts of his creatures for their love and loyalty in an eternal struggle. *That* was to come while Pontius Pilate was Procurator of Judea.

Bishop Bruce R. Baxter tells of speaking to a man about God upon hearing that the man had just been notified that his son had been killed in action in the last world war. "Where was God that night when my boy was being killed?" snapped the anguished father in the condition and mood of Job of old. "He was in the same place as when his own Son was being killed," was the Christian reply Baxter was able to make. Among the good who suffer undeserved is God himself.

CHAPTER 9

Who Do You Say that I Am?

Now when Jesus came into the district of Caesarea Philippi, he asked his disciples, "Who do men say that the Son of man is?" And they said, "Some say John the Baptist, others say Elijah, and others Jeremiah or one of the prophets." He said to them, "But who do you say that I am?" Simon Peter replied, "You are the Christ, the Son of the living God." And Jesus answered him, "Blessed are you, Simon Bar-Jona! For flesh and blood has not revealed this to you, but my Father who is in heaven. And I tell you, you are Peter, and on this rock I will build my church, and the powers of death shall not prevail against it." (Matt. 16:13-18)

God, as we have seen, asks searching questions. The Bible is evidence of this fact. Time and again in its pages is left the record that someone, at some time and in some manner, has known himself to have been interrogated by the Eternal. God presses men to face basic issues of life, and by posing to them a question or a decision he obliges them to accept a fact or to take a stand. Whether these questions have been preserved for us in inspired myth, as in the stories of Adam and Cain, or in the prophets' chronicles of his inner experiences as with Amos and Hosea, or in the fine awareness of literary minds like those that produced the dramas of Job and Jonah, the questions are there, and they abide. They leap the bounds of their time and place in history. They transcend the matter as to whether their contexts in scripture are factual or fictional. They have forced themselves on the consciences of those who have read them through the centuries. And they confront us today.

Thus far the questions we have considered, real and pointed as they have been, involve something less than the whole of a man's life. Authentic as they are, and deep as they probe, they are all overshadowed and encompassed in a bigger inquiry of God, certainly the most important one of all. It was addressed to living men of flesh and blood by an audible male voice in a certain town on a certain day. It is a question that divides the world—but not by setting nation against nation, race against race, or class against class. Rather, it sets a man against his father, a daughter against her mother, and a daughter-in-law against her mother-in-law—and a man against his former self. The question was asked by Jesus of Nazareth. It was addressed in this instance to Simon, son of Jona, and possibly to others of the twelve who were present at the time.

First, Jesus asked, "Who do men say that the Son of man is?" He asked his disciples to tell him what people were saying about him. Now that is a relatively easy question.

Who Do You Say that I Am?

If a close friend asks us what people say about him, we will usually tell him. It does not greatly disturb us to report what people are saying—what the latest rumor or gossip is. We might shield a friend from adverse comment about him, but we are happy to share good reports. So the disciples, we can imagine, were in no distress when Jesus asked them who other people said that he was. The reports were really flattering, or they considered them so. So the disciples told Jesus that some considered him to be a "reincarnation" of John the Baptist; others thought he was Elijah come back to earth again, or Jeremiah, or one of the other prophets—estimable personages all. Of course the disciples may have been hedging. They might have been shielding Jesus from the harsh names some peoples were calling him, if they knew. But it didn't really matter. For Jesus' first question was really only a setup for the big one he intended to ask.

Looking squarely at the men who knew him better than any other men knew him, he asked them a question that they could not evade: "But who do *you* say that I am?" It was Peter who blurted out what all of them probably thought: "You are the Christ, the Son of the living God." The gospel writers differ as to what Jesus' reaction was. It is Matthew who reports that Jesus was pleased with the answer Peter had made. The Master replied that Peter's response was what God wanted—*or close enough*. And upon it Jesus promised to build a church against which the powers of darkness would not prevail. Whichever gospel account we read, Jesus put the question and Peter gave the answer. And it is upon that response which the apostle made that the Christian Church has in fact been built.

Now what is so important about that question, and that answer? Was Jesus conscious of rank and jealous of title? Was he, like oriental despots of old—and some functionaries of today—touchy about his title? Jesus' contemporary, the emperor Nero, demanded that his attendants call him "Divinity." The Pope is properly addressed only as "Your Holiness." The Archbishop of Canterbury is to be addressed as "Your Grace." Several years ago when King George VI of England was in failing health, a solicitous British commoner asked Princess Margaret, "How is your father?" The princess coldly drew the line at which the formalities of rank must be observed. "I presume you mean His Majesty," she replied icily. (Not quite so well authenticated are the instances in which a sailor in the second world war unexpectedly found himself addressed by Admiral Halsey. "Yes, Your Flagship," the flustered lad stammered. And again, a tipsy defendant is reported to have addressed the judge before whom he was on trial, not as "Your Honor," but as "Your Courtship.") Is this sort of thing the reason for Jesus' question, and the sanction for Peter's answer? Just to entertain this idea is to reject it as ridiculous. "Not every one who says to me, 'Lord, Lord,' shall enter the kingdom of heaven, but he who does the will of my Father who is in heaven," Jesus once said. (Matt. 7:21.) And again: "Why do you call me 'Lord, Lord,' and not do what I tell you?" (Luke 6:46.) The trappings of honor meant nothing at all to Jesus.

Or does Jesus' place in history and in the esteem of men

depend in some way upon a certain formulation of his identity? Does addressing him in honorific terms add to his goodness or grandeur? Does it commend him to those who would otherwise scorn him or ignore him? Does it make him stand out in the ancient world where such titles were commonplace, or in the modern world where such titles are suspect? Can we add an inch to his stature by what we claim him to be, or subtract an inch from it by what we do not claim him to be? Does the Church create the Christ by bestowing titles upon him, or destroy him by withholding them? Again to ask the question is to answer it negatively.

Or, are we to be saved or damned by our opinions upon a historical matter? Jesus of Nazareth was a figure in human history just as Caesar Augustus and Napoleon were. Our New Testament is the whole of the records of his life. Some say that it is entirely sufficient—that the case is proved that he was divine. Others doubt the adequacy of the record to prove what they claim. Competent historians sometimes disagree, I am told. They disagree radically on matters as recent as the Civil War. They disagree in their estimates of the stature of Theodore Roosevelt and Harry Truman. Are you and I to be saved or damned by our opinions on a matter of history that occurred some two thousand years ago? Is it such an opinion—such a school of thought— which is the foundation of the Christian church? Again the answer is no.

Furthermore, the title for Jesus which Peter used is not precise in meaning, nor is it theologically definitive. The word "Christ" is the Greek word for the Hebrew word

97

"Messiah," which means the anointed one. It meant different things to different Jews in Jesus' day, which may account for Jesus' reluctance to be called by that title publicly. (Mark 8:27-30 and Luke 9:18-21.) It means very little to anyone in our day except as a synonym for Jesus himself. The term "Son of God" is not an exact term in its meaning either. To some it means conceived by the Holy Ghost. But it does not *necessarily* mean that. The disciples, James and John, were known as sons of thunder, and the name Barnabas means son of encouragement. And John wrote to his fellow Christians, "beloved, *we* are God's children now" (I John 3:2). Clearly, the term "Son of God" could mean any of several things. What then is so important about Jesus' question, and Peter's answer?

It is important because Jesus was such a one that we cannot ignore him, nor be neutral toward him. His very presence among men forced them to reveal themselves, to declare themselves, and to commit themselves. Who do *you* say Jesus is? A fool? A good, but deluded, man? A wise teacher who was somehow fraudulently deified by twelve Palestinian peasants and a renegade rabbi from Tarsus, who somehow made it stick for two thousand years? Or was he in some singular sense, as Peter put it, "the Son of the Living God"? Think well. This question does not ask your opinion on some historical incident; *it asks your faith on the nature of the universe in which you live*. It is not to be answered from the top of your head, but from the depths of your being where your central loyalties are formed. It affects not your denominational affiliation, but your identification with the Christian faith and your participation in the Christian hope. It controls not just a few of your habits, but the basic orientation of your life. And no one can answer it for you but you. Biblical scholars won't settle it—as Biblical scholars—even if they were to come into possession of the original copy of every book in the New Testament. Scientists won't settle it—as scientists—though their instruments of research be sharpened a hundredfold. Every man answers this one for himself—as a man.

Essentially, the question is where we look to find God, and whether we know him when we see him. In his play *Sweet Bird of Youth,* Tennessee Williams has one of his characters say, "I believe that the long silence of God, the absolute speechlessness of Him, is a long, long and awful thing that the whole world is lost because of; I think it's yet to be broken to any man living or any yet lived on earth, no exceptions." [1] Here is made explicit the fundamental denial that God has shown himself in Jesus, and that Jesus spoke for anyone but himself. One who takes this position must at least entertain the possibility that the fact is not God's silence but his own deafness, and that he would not know divinity if he saw it. And it is precisely at this point that one proceeds by faith or not at all. Here, I believe, rather than at any other point in Christian tradition or dogma, one makes the leap of faith, or the leap of denial, that determines his basic relationship to the universe in which he lives. It is a wager, and the stake is one's soul.

Peter's response—and it is the response that is important,

[1] © 1959 by Two Rivers Enterprises, Inc. Reprinted by permission of New Directions.

rather than the verbal formulation of his reply—was that Jesus was the Son of the living God. Henceforth for Peter the invisible God was to wear the face of Jesus of Nazareth, and to speak with the Nazarene's voice. Henceforth for Peter the "silence of Eternity" was "interpreted by love." Henceforth he lived in a kingdom which had begun to come, but was not yet fully here. Henceforth he marched to different music, served in a different army, and looked to a different victory. He read the whole universe differently from then on. The same is true of all who have shared the apostles' faith through the centuries.

Somewhere in one of his books, Walter Marshall Horton told of watching for the first time a production of John Drinkwater's play *Abraham Lincoln*. As he watched the moving figure of Lincoln suffering with the nation he was seeking to save, and rising above the tides of bitter hatred that threatened to wash it down, and meeting "with malice toward none and charity for all" the animosity and anger that were directed at him personally, he, Horton, felt himself suffused by an affirmation of faith. This, he felt deep within him, is a reflection of reality. This is an image of the Eternal God weeping and working with his children to save them from themselves. It was an experience and an affirmation of this kind—with greater intensity and less ambiguity —that the living Jesus must have evoked from the big fisherman. It was an affirmation of this kind that Jesus on the cross evoked from the tough Roman army officer who stood guard at the foot of the cross. (Matt. 27:54; Mark 15:39.) It is an affirmation of this kind that has been evoked from the hearts of millions of men through the centuries as they have become acquainted with Jesus of Nazareth. Here in Jesus is the supreme image of God's love for us all. The spirit of this man of Nazareth is the spirit of the "Eternal God whose power upholds both flower and flaming star." Jesus' compassion is the divine compassion. His will for men is God's will for men. Jesus' self-giving unto us is God giving himself unto us.

In Peter's confession of faith, then, we deal not with a trite formula or a superfluous dogma, but with an exciting adventure of the mind. Once one has, in faith, identified Jesus with God, the practical implications for his life are profound. It makes the mind of Jesus—insofar as it can be ascertained and translated from first century contexts into twentieth century contexts—morally authoritative. No longer does he think of Jesus' teaching as beautiful ideals and lofty sentiments. They become for him his map of reality. He tries to obey Jesus insofar as he knows how— not because he thinks it is nice, but because he believes it to be wise. Jesus' commandments do not seem to him the lovely thing to do, but the smart thing to do—Jesus being who he was. Indeed, Jesus rarely, if ever, appealed to men's idealism in ethical matters; he appealed to their desire to survive in a universe whose moral structure he revealed to them. The usual form of Jesus' ethical teaching was that our obligations derive naturally from the character of God and the universe which he had made. The *ought* derives from the *is*. Or as Jesus himself put it, to do what he commanded is to build on rock; to do otherwise is to build upon sand. These things become the world view of one who con-

cludes, on faith, that Jesus was the Son of God and therefore represented God authentically.

And although one who has committed himself to the
idea that Jesus reveals reality does not depend upon subsequent opinion for his faith, he does, of course, welcome
the confirmation which abundantly occurs. The most remarkable statement of its kind that I have ever come upon
was made by Dr. James Tucker Fisher. He was a psychi-
atrist who had studied under Freud in Vienna and practiced
in Los Angeles for fifty years before writing at the age
of eighty-seven:

I believe the following to be true; if you were to take the
sum total of all the authoritative articles ever written by the
most qualified of psychologists and psychiatrists on the subject
of mental hygiene—if you were to combine them, and refine
them, and cleave out the excess verbiage—if you were to take
the whole of the meat and none of the parsley, and if you
were to have these unadulterated bits of pure scientific knowledge concisely expressed by the most capable of living poets,
you would have an awkward and incomplete summation of the
Sermon on the Mount.[2]

One who has wagered his soul that Jesus speaks for God
expects such vindication—slowly and partially in his lifetime, but surely and wholly in the long run. And he gets
it, although it may come for him, as it did for his Lord, on
the far side of a cross. So believing, his morale remains high
and his personality whole in the face of the adversities and

[2] *A Few Buttons Missing* (New York: J. B. Lippincott Co., 1951),
p. 273.

ambiguities of his own lifetime. He is able to dare, and love, and persevere, and wait. In the fellowship of others who have made this wager—which is the church—he finds support and encouragement when he wants it, forgiveness when he needs it, and reminding when he begins to forget. And he remembers that this faith he holds is the rock upon which is built the church against which the powers of evil shall not prevail. Who do you say Jesus is? Your answer to this divine inquiry is the most far-reaching response you shall make to the mystery which is our human life.

CHAPTER 10

Was It Not Necessary
That the Christ Should Suffer?

And he said to them, "O foolish men, and slow of heart to believe all that the prophets have spoken! Was it not necessary that the Christ should suffer these things and enter into his glory?" And beginning with Moses and all the prophets, he interpreted to them in all the scriptures the things concerning himself. (Luke 24:25-27)

Among the first followers of Jesus was a man named Cleopas. He missed total obscurity by the narrowest of margins. His name is mentioned only once in only one book of the New Testament, the Gospel of Luke. Yet it is an important happening in which he found himself caught up. He was among those who saw the risen Christ. More particularly, Luke credits Cleopas with being the first to hear a question that has occupied Christian minds for twenty centuries. It is a singularly perplexing and searching question that leads one's mind toward profound insights into the nature of himself, his world, and the ways of God in the world. Hence we attribute the question to divine origin, both in its occurrence in the thinking of the ancient Christian community, and as it agitates us to do some theological thinking in our own day. Surely it is one of the inquiries by which God has moved the reflective mind toward himself.

The circumstances surrounding this question, as Luke records them, are these. On the first day of the week following the crucifixion of Jesus, Cleopas and another disciple were walking from Jerusalem to the village of Emmaus about seven miles away. As they walked they naturally were discussing the tragic blow dealt to their hopes on Calvary's hill—and God's strange reversal of the tragedy, which already was beginning its transforming work upon the disciples' vision. While the two thus walked and talked, they found themselves joined by another whom they did not then recognize. The stranger asked them what they were talking about. Then Cleopas, with irritation and unconscious irony, asked the stranger if he were the only visitor to Jerusalem who didn't know the things that had just happened there. The stranger pressed further, "What things?" Cleopas replied, "Concerning Jesus of Nazareth, who was a prophet mighty in deed and word before God and all the people, and how our chief priests and rulers delivered him up to be condemned to death and crucified him." Cleopas then told further of the visit of the women to the empty tomb, and their vision of angels who said that Jesus was alive. Then from the mysterious presence came this reply: "O foolish men, and slow of heart to believe all that the prophets have spoken! Was it not necessary that the Christ should suffer these things and enter into his glory?" And beginning with Moses and all the prophets, he interpreted to them in all the scriptures the things concerning himself.

Was it not necessary that the Christ should suffer? Here, you see, was a question that the disciples had to face. The Messiah, executed like a common criminal, was not an idea that came easily to Jews. The fact that their beloved Master had been scorned and repudiated was something that had to be thought through by the disciples. The Son of the living God, nailed to a cross, was a contradiction too bold to be brushed off. As Paul declared: "Christ crucified, a stumbling block to Jews and folly to Gentiles." And, we must add, a devastating blow to those who had loved him dearly, and believed upon him. "We *had hoped*," said Cleopas in a forlorn confession heavy with the past tense of shattered dreams, "that he *was* the one to redeem Israel."

Into this sullen context was interjected this electric question. It was an inquiry from God himself that acted as a catalyst upon the minds of the early disciples. And it has been making Christians think ever since. "Was it not necessary that the Christ should suffer?" Notice how the question is worded, and the kind of answer it suggests. During the second world war, Uncle Sam was trying to save gasoline, rubber, and train accommodations for military uses. All over the country there appeared signs asking the would-be traveler about to embark upon a frivolous journey, "Is this trip necessary?" It was meant to evoke the answer "No," and to shame Americans into staying at home. (Inevitably, of course, bomber crews overseas painted on the noses of their planes about to take off on a bombing mission, "Is *this* trip necessary?" Again the answer implied in sardonic jest is "No.") When we ask a friend whether it is necessary to dress for dinner, say, we are inquiring solely for information on a relatively minor matter, and it does not really make very much difference to us whether the answer be yes or no. But notice how different is the tone and content of the question which the mysterious presence put to Cleopas. It calls upon all who hear it to recognize the inherent certainty, the inevitability, that the divine love could become flesh and live among us only at the cost of suffering to itself.

It was necessary that the Christ should suffer—men being what they are. We do not take kindly to those who threaten our privileges. Jesus assured himself trouble when he drove out of the temple those who profiteered upon the worshipers' needs, saying, "It is written, 'My house shall be called a house of prayer'; but you make it a den of robbers" (Matt. 21:13). He assured himself trouble when he played down the formal and legalistic side of religion, and stressed justice, mercy, and faith—as had the persecuted prophets before him. This not only earns one the enmity of high priests and Pharisees, but it makes religion painfully relevant to everyone's daily dealings. Nor do we take kindly to one who makes us think. Jesus was certain to create bitterness and disappointment in proclaiming a kingdom which was not only "not of the world," but was to be put ahead of the concrete material pursuits which are of this world. He aroused suspicion and hostility, moreover, by treating Samaritans as though they had the same claim on the divine mercies as Jews.

Having aroused both official and unofficial leadership against him, the remainder of his road was certain to be hard. He became, in due time, a prisoner of the military, who made sport of him. The soldiers who tortured him were certainly bored stiff, and probably drunk. He was tried by the all-too-familiar process of hurling accusations and rumor at him faster than they could possibly be refuted. (And the corresponding assumption that where there is smoke there is probably fire!) He was sacrificed to save a Roman procurator from facing a riot that would surely have cost him his position. He was lynched, with a few gestures toward legality, by a city rabble.

We mortals don't know what to do with pure goodness when we see it. It confuses us, frightens us, and embarrasses us. Let us consider ourselves lucky that we aren't the generation that had to deal with Jesus in the flesh. Let us be content that no Pilate asked of us what he should do with Jesus. Stanley Rowland has suggested what our more blasé generation might typically do under the circumstances:

> If Christ should come today, we would
> Not crucify, not curse or praise
> Nor stand aghast. We would instead
> Shave him clean and go to Brooks,
> Fit him with a hat from Knox,
> Buy him shirts by Hathaway,
> Equip him with the best advice
> And script, then put him on TV—
> He'd find a sponsor soon, and after

> Tea he might provoke a sigh;
> Indeed, why should we crucify? [1]

We being what we are, it was inevitable that the Christ should suffer.

And it was necessary that the Christ should suffer—he being what he was. Any great heart suffers in our world. Indeed anyone who loves deeply lays himself open to grief and pain and disappointment. And Jesus loved more widely and deeply than any other has ever loved. He loved with a scope and intensity like that of the heavenly Father. What parent does not suffer with, and for, and because of, the suffering of his children? Even when the little rascals bring it upon themselves—perhaps most so then—a parent suffers with his children. Raise that to the nth degree, and we begin to understand what the Christ bore.

The most memorized verse in the Bible—unfortunately because it is the shortest one—is "Jesus wept." Those curious enough to look into the context of the verse discover why Jesus wept. He had just learned that his friend Lazarus had died. (John 11.) Now most of us would weep under such circumstances. We would weep in sorrow and loss because we would miss our friend. We would weep in sympathy and in empathy with the family of the one who had died, sharing their loss and loneliness. But this is not the only time that Jesus wept. As he drew near to the city of Jerusalem on "Palm Sunday," he wept again for that city full of strangers. He wept for it because of what it was doing to itself—because of its lostness, its spiritual barren-

---

[1] "Speaking Jesuswise," *The Christian Century,* April 2, 1958.

ness and blindness. He wept because the people who lived there did not know the things that make for their peace, and because of the fate that would surely come to them unless they had a change of heart and values. He wept, not for himself, but for the city.

Luke records that, while walking with Cleopas and his friend, Jesus "interpreted to them in all the scriptures the things concerning himself." Surely among these things which made the hearts of Cleopas and his friend burn within them while he "opened to them the scriptures" was the Second Isaiah's picture of the suffering servant of the Lord: "He was despised and rejected by men; a man of sorrows, and acquainted with grief. . . . Surely he has borne our griefs and carried our sorrows." Jesus suffered because of who he was and what he was. He suffered because of his Godlike tenderness for a lost and sinning humanity.

It was necessary that the Christ should suffer, moreover, God's purpose being what it is—to touch men's hard hearts and soften them—to reach men's cold hearts and win them —to jolt us out of our self-centeredness, self-preoccupation, and self-pity. The crucifixion of Jesus will do just that if we open our eyes and minds to it.

William Inge has drawn profoundly upon Christian insight and symbolism in his recent play, *The Dark at the Top of the Stairs*. The play is the story of a quarreling, unhappy family in a small Oklahoma town in the early 1920's. All of the members of the Rubin Flood family were wrapped up in self-pity, insecurity, and fear. Reenie Flood, the sixteen-year-old daughter, accepted a blind date for a party at the country club for the daughter of the local society leader. Reenie's date turned out to be Sammy Golden-baum, a sensitive Jewish lad who for all practical purposes was an unwanted orphan. At the dance, Reenie became embarrassed because no other boy cut in to dance with her. She didn't want Sammy to see that she was not popular with the local boys, so she fled to the girls' powder room, and left Sammy to dance with the hostess' daughter. The hostess was a snob, and she had also had too much to drink. She strode out to Sammy on the dance floor, and in a loud voice delivered herself of her opinions of Jews and their place—which, she said, was not in the country club and particularly not dancing with her daughter. To Sammy, mother Flood reflected later, "she probably sounded like the voice of the world." Deeply hurt, Sammy tried to find Reenie, his date, who was still in hiding. Being unable to find her, he left the dance and later took his life. Upon learning of the tragedy later, Reenie in shock and grief reflected upon her behavior and the subsequent events of the evening. "He asked for me . . . for me," she sobbed. "The only time anyone ever *wanted* me, or *needed* me, in my entire life. And I wasn't there. I didn't stop once to think of . . . Sammy. I've always thought I was the only person in the world who had any feelings at all." [2] This was the beginning of insight in Reenie—and in other members of the Flood family—that began remaking them, and restoring them to mutual concern and mutual support of

[2] Act III, p. 294. Copyright, 1945, as an unpublished work by William Motter Inge under the title *Farther Off from Heaven*. Copyright 1958 by William Inge. Reprinted by permission of Random House, Inc.

each other in their respective needs. The undeserved suffering of a Jewish boy began the redemption of a family.

Christian faith has never been content, of course, to see in the crucifixion of Jesus simply the death of an innocent Jew. We see in his death not merely the martyrdom of another prophet—although that has its healing power. Christians from the first to the present see in Christ's crucifixion the involvement of God himself in the painful consequences of human sin. When Christ was "wounded for our transgressions" we perceive that God himself suffered, and suffers, on our behalf. Upon him was the chastisement that makes us whole. Christ suffered because God was in Christ reconciling the world unto himself.

When General Eisenhower was running for the presidency of the United States in 1952, he promised the American people that if he were elected he would "go to Korea" where American troops were tied down in a nasty, bloody, little war. He was elected, and he kept his promise and went to Korea. The American people were deeply grateful, and deeply moved, that their highest officer would personally visit the front where their boys were fighting and dying. To be sure, the President traveled in comfort, and was protected by all the vigilance and power that the secret service and the armed forces of the United States could throw around a single individual. Even so, the fact that he went at all touched all of us deeply. My soul, how much greater the redeeming power to move us from pettiness and selfishness and sin when God himself visited the front where we fight and die, "lowly and riding on an ass"—and was killed there. By his stripes we are healed.

CHAPTER 11

Have You Believed
Because You Have Seen?

*Now Thomas, one of the twelve, called the
Twin, was not with them when Jesus came.
So the other disciples told him, "We have seen
the Lord." But he said to them, "Unless I see
in his hands the print of the nails, and place
my finger in the mark of the nails, and place
my hand in his side, I will not believe."*

*Eight days later, his disciples were again in the
house, and Thomas was with them. The doors
were shut, but Jesus came and stood among
them, and said, "Peace be with you." Then
he said to Thomas, "Put your finger here, and
see my hands; and put out your hand, and
place it in my side; do not be faithless, but
believing." Thomas answered him, "My Lord
and my God!" Jesus said to him "Have you
believed because you have seen me? Blessed
are those who have not seen and yet believe."*
(John 20:24-29)

It is surprising how skeptical the first disciples were. We sometimes assume that they were superstitious oafs living in constant expectation of a miracle. Scripture supports no such picture of them. They were men of their times, to be sure. They lived in a prescientific age. They thought that sickness was caused by demons rather than by bacteria. They believed that heaven was up, and hell was down. But on the whole they looked upon life with realistic eyes. There was very little in the lives of Palestinian fishermen to encourage fantasy and mysticism. They did not wait upon Jesus with the gullible expectation that the devotees of modern faith healers, or mediums, wait upon their idol. Indeed we read again and again of the disciples' doubts that Jesus had risen from the dead. Matthew in describing one of Jesus' postresurrection appearances, says of the disciples "and when they saw him they worshiped him: but some doubted." (28:17.) In Mark we read the following description of the disciples' reactions to Mary Magdalene's story of seeing the risen Lord: "But when they heard that he was alive, and had been seen by her, they would not believe it" (16:11). Luke tells us that "returning from the tomb they [the women] told all this to the eleven and to all the rest. . . . but these words seemed to them an idle tale, and they did not believe them" (24:9-11).

But it is, of course, doubting Thomas whom we know best. He would not even believe the other apostles when they told him that they had seen the Lord after his crucifixion. "Unless *I* see in his hands the print of the nails . . . and place *my* hand in his side, I will not believe," he said.

Thomas demanded an impression upon his own eyeballs. He demanded to poke his own finger in the holes left by the iron spikes and spear. John tells us that Jesus granted to Thomas his request, and that this evoked from Thomas the exclamation of belief, "My Lord and my God!"

I am aware of the difficulties that biblical scholars, not to mention common sense materialists, have with this and all other stories of Jesus' resurrection. They have difficulties taking them at face value, and equally great difficulties getting around them altogether. But notice here in this improbable sounding story this hard-as-nails question. In the scriptural narrative it was addressed by the risen Christ to the apostle Thomas. In its import, it is addressed from the depths of mystery to every thoughtful man. *"Have you believed, because you have seen me?* Blessed are those who have not seen, and yet believe." What do you believe, and why do you believe it? Here indeed is an inquiry of God. It is addressed not just to a single apostle twenty centuries ago; it is also addressed to you and me today. Do you believe only because you have seen?

Well, what do we believe, and why do we believe it? In part, we do believe what we have seen. "Seeing is believing," we say. And "one picture is worth a thousand words" has become a weary old cliché which is nevertheless at least partially true. We trust our eyes more than we do our other four senses. Why, I don't know. A dog trusts his nose more than his eyes. A deer trusts his ears more than his eyes. Other forms of life proceed mostly by their sense of touch. We rely, of course, on all of our senses, but the eye is king. And indeed much of what we know and believe

115

does come to us via our eyes. We build telescopes to extend our sight upward and outward. We build microscopes to extend our eyesight downward and inward. We use ultraviolet and infrared light to extend the range of things visible to us, and X rays to see through this too too solid flesh. All of this rewards us with an abundance of useful knowledge that is not available to less technical peoples.

But the eye can be fooled. Any draftsman can draw or assemble a design that will make our eyes mislead us entirely. We call it an optical illusion. On a television program recently I watched a young man do sleight of hand. He held a ringing alarm clock in his hand, covered it with a cloth, gently flipped the cloth, and made the clock, jangling bell and all, vanish into the clear and silent air. I saw it with my own eyes. But I don't believe it. With a competent television cameraman for assistance, even a mediocre magician ought to be able to bring a live elephant to pass before our eyes, and dissolve him into nothing just as quickly. A prize-winning Japanese film of recent years is entitled *Rashomon*. In it the same crime is witnessed by different participants. All saw the same events—and yet no two saw the same events. Interest, desire, and different perspectives and capacities for sight all entered in. One is led to question whether the eye ever reports the truth.

How far could a child go in school who believed only what he saw with his own eyes? He would believe nothing told to him by his teacher or by others. He would learn no history, and no philosophy. He would learn only such geography as he had been able to see from an automobile window. He could learn a piddling speck of natural science, and even less of social science. His mind would remain forever impoverished by his ridiculous demand that he personally experience all things with his senses before he would believe them. Life obliges us as a matter of course to accept as true many things beyond the scope of our personal sense experience. "Unless I see . . . and place my finger!" Actually only a fragment of what we really believe comes to us via impact upon our own eyeballs and finger tips. As Paul Johnson says, "What superstition is more deadly than to insist there is nothing beyond what we have known?" "Blessed are those who have not seen, and yet believe," said Jesus.

We rely, of course, upon the testimony of others, and upon our reason, as well as upon our senses. To be sure, much of natural science is built up of experiments which anyone could duplicate if he wanted to, and if he knew how to go about it. But that is not true of our knowledge of history, nor of any of the complex human events of the past. Here we must of necessity rely upon records from the period, such as they are. We must rely upon the comments of those who were there at the time. We must hear interpreters, old and new. We must seek the opinion of the most qualified authorities whom we can find. Then, ultimately, we must weigh all these things in the balances of our own judgment, and combine them with other things that we know or believe to be true. Then we must make up our minds as to what is the truth. In short, we believe many things because our reason leads us to them. All that we can know or believe of the historical figure of Jesus comes to us in this way. But it is far more than the naked testimony of our own senses.

Last summer, I was driving home from a trip out of town. As I approached the city limits, I noticed that trees were down across the road, and street lights were out, and the streets strewn with river patterns of sand and gravel. Friends told me that there had been a summer storm, but they really didn't need to. I had already concluded that. Even though I had not seen the storm, nor a streak of lightning, nor a blackened cloud in the sky, I saw the evidence of their having been there. The risen Christ, in whom we believe, we know as I know that summer storm. We did not feel the winds of Pentecost, but we know that Christ's smitten and broken disciples were blown upright again, and became sturdy oaks. We did not feel the earthquake upon that first day of the week after the crucifixion. But we cannot doubt that the early Christians shook Rome to its foundations. Justin Martyr, in a letter written to the Emperor Antoninus Pius around the middle of the second century, said, "Twelve men went out from Jerusalem into the world, and they were ignorant men, unable to speak; but by the power of God they told every race of men that they were sent by Christ to teach all men the word of God. And we who formerly slew one another not only do not make war against our enemies, but for the sake of not telling lies or deceiving those who examine us, gladly die confessing Christ." [1] We did not see the angel at the empty tomb whose appearance was like lightning. But in Christ's name,

[1] *Apology,* XXXIX.

and under the influence of his spirit, we know that angels of light and mercy have gone throughout the world to the darkest corners of men's suffering and ignorance.

The most convincing evidence in scripture for the resurrection of Jesus is not the story of Thomas seeing his Lord and touching his palms and side. The most compelling account is the behavior of Peter and John, recorded in the book of Acts. They were arrested for preaching the risen Jesus, and healing in his name. They were brought before the "supreme court" of the Jewish nation, and commanded to do it no more. But this time they were not cowed by the power and threats of officialdom, as they had been when Jesus was on trial before them. They said they could not keep quiet about what they had seen and knew. Of the officials, Luke records, "Now when they saw the boldness of Peter and John, and perceived that they were uneducated and common men, they wondered; and they recognized that they had been with Jesus (Acts 4:13). It is what Jesus did, and does, to and through common men of the first century and the twentieth that convinces me that he lives. "With great power the apostles gave their testimony to the resurrection of the Lord Jesus, and great grace was upon them all." (Acts 4:33.)

We are not among the few who have been privileged to see the living Christ with our own eyes. But we are among the many who know the evidence that he returned with power into the affairs of men. Still today, he wins the assent of men's minds, captures their allegiance, constrains their consciences, fires their imaginations, directs their wills, and steels their faltering nerve. He does these things not as a

119

phantom of memory, but as a compelling contemporary. His resurrection commends itself to our judgment and belief through these observations of his presence among us, though we shall never place our fingers in his side.

But beyond the things which we believe through our senses, through the testimony of others, and through our reason, there is a depth of belief which can only be called faith. It is not contrary to sense and reason, but it involves more of the self. James Gould Cozzens must have had this in mind when he called certain intellectual beliefs "no more than figments of the reason, never the realities of feeling." Indeed, our reason often appears to be a fragile construction, floating on turbulent tides of feeling. Thus Chad Walsh was led to observe, with considerable evidence to back him up, that "man is a rational animal only under optimum conditions." In reality, the whole bearing of our lives may be determined by deep desires and fears and hates and loves. And the reasons we give for our beliefs and behavior may in truth be largely rationalizations for some deeper commitments and constraints within us.

Certainly, unless our religion has this visceral dimension to it, as well as its intellectual dimension, it remains forever a mere figment of the reason. Indeed, the things we believe at this profound level of our beings may properly be called our real religion. It will be a fundamental loyalty, or a hope, which we cannot discuss altogether dispassionately. It will be a subject upon which we can never remain entirely cool. Probably the American philosopher, John Dewey, is about as far as one can get from the traditional idea of religious faith. Dewey believed that all truth was derived from experience. The greatest obstacles to finding truth, in his opinion, were traditions and authorities of various kinds which shackled men's minds. He felt that everything would turn out all right if men and women, society in general, were set free to apply their intelligence to solving their problems. Their goals and values would satisfactorily emerge before them as they went along. The late Edwin E. Aubrey used to tell his classes of an occasion when Dewey was defending this viewpoint against some who did not share his optimism. How did he know, they asked the doughty old intellectual giant, that everything would be worked out by society if only the traditional shackles and authorities were removed from men's thinking? Dewey repeated himself in slightly different words, but the questioners kept pressing in upon him. "Well," the old philosopher finally growled, "I suppose that democracy is my religion."

Precisely! At some point, everyone must growl, "This is my religion." This is my faith. This is my commitment. This is my hope. This is my major premise—my leap in the dark—the inescapable wager of my soul. My other beliefs ultimately grow from it. This quality certainly characterized the belief of the apostles. Peter, after the crucifixion, thought of the magnificent, tender, compelling figure of Jesus. And then he thought of the sodden nothingness of death. And then the meaning of the resurrection burst upon him with clarity and fire. "It was not possible," cried Peter at white heat, "for *him* to be held by *it*." (Acts 2:24.) And nineteen centuries later, an English army chaplain, also at white heat, cried:

How is it proved?
It isn't proved, you fool; it can't be proved.
How can you prove a victory before
It's won? How can you prove a man who leads
To be a leader worth the following,
Unless you follow to the death, and out
Beyond mere death, which is not anything
But Satan's lie upon eternal life?
Well—God's my leader, and I hold that he
Is good, and strong enough to work his plan
And purpose out to its appointed end.

. . . .

... I bet my life on beauty, truth,
And love! not abstract, but incarnate truth;
Not beauty's passing shadow, but its self,
Its very self made flesh—love realized.
I bet my life on Christ, Christ crucified.
Aye risen, and alive forevermore.[2]

Do you believe only because you have seen? Blessed are those who have not seen, and yet believe.

[2] G. A. Studdert-Kennedy, "The Great Wager." By permission of Harper and Bros.

CHAPTER 12

Do You Love Me?

When they had finished breakfast, Jesus said
to Simon Peter, "Simon, son of John, do you
love me more than these?" He said to him,
"Yes, Lord; you know that I love you." He
said to him, "Feed my lambs."

(John 21:15-16)

Peter said, "I am going
fishing." Some of the other disciples said, "We will go with
you." So they did. They went out and got into the boat;
but that night they caught nothing. (John 21:1-3.) Fishing,
to the apostles, was not the recreation that it is to some of
us. It was their work. It was the occupaion at which Jesus
had first found them. It was their former way of life—their
status quo ante. Peter and some of the other disciples decided to go back to it. Or perhaps they didn't exactly decide,
but rather just drifted back to it, or slipped back into it. And
this was despite the fact that Christ had risen, and they
knew that he had risen. Already he had manifested himself
to them alive, after he had been crucified. They had already
experienced him as a living presence in their midst—victor

over death. Yet Peter said that he was going fishing—and for fish. And the other disciples, who often took their direction from Peter's initiative, said that they were going with him.

This is the spiritual context of a story which appears in the Gospel of John. As day was breaking, the weary fishermen saw the figure of Jesus on the beach of the Sea of Galilee where they had seen him so often before. Perhaps it was near the spot at which he had first called James and John from their nets to follow him. Now, as they worked the night shift, they found their Lord near them again. And when they took time off for breakfast, they found that Jesus again was their host, as he had been in the upper room. It was a characteristic experience of the first followers that they felt their risen Lord closest to them when they broke bread together. As another gospel writer described this same kind of experience in a different setting, "He was known to them in the breaking of bread" (Luke 24:35).

Then it was that Simon Peter found himself faced with a question. It was a question put to him by the uncomfortable presence of the living Christ, with him there on the beach. And what an inquiry it was. In a sense it was plaintive. But it was authenticated by the majestic tenderness of it, and it reflects the infinite forgiveness out of which the heavenly Father addresses his children. Surely it came into Peter's mind from the Divine Mind, and as such it was urgent and imperious, for all its gentleness. "Simon, son of John, do you love me more than these?"

My soul, think of what Christ could have asked Peter—justly, fairly, understandably—on this occasion. "Well

Simon, son of John," he could have asked, "what happened to *you*? Where was my Rock on the morning after our last Passover meal together when my enemies beset me around, and I was betrayed into their hands to be slain? Where were you when I needed you most—when I could have used the strong shoulder of a faithful friend in my human plight? Do you remember your loud boast a few minutes before when you vowed that even though all the others fell away, you would not? Did you not promise that even if you must die with me, you would not deny me? I told you that you would deny me that very night, remember? And you did. Three times while warming your hands at our enemies' fire you denied that you even knew me. Did you have to be so vehement? Well, Simon, son of John, what do you have to say for yourself?" These are such questions as we think would have been appropriate to ask of Peter. Peter had undoubtedly asked them of himself, over and over again. There are a thousand such questions you and I would feel free to ask of a fickle friend, or an undependable assistant, or an unfaithful mate, or an erring child. These are the human questions one naturally asks when he has been wronged. These are the kind of just inquiries, logical moral questions, one has the right to ask when he has been let down or betrayed.

But they are not the questions that the victorious Christ asked of the penitent fisherman. He asked one question only—though he asked it repeatedly. "Simon, son of John, do you love me? More important to me than your past vows, your present beliefs, your resolutions for the future—granting you your inconstancy and your weakness—in spite of

your record of failure and of cowardice—*do you love me?*"
That is all that the risen Christ asked Simon Peter. It
reflects, I believe, what God most wants to know of each
of us. How thankful we may be that *this* is what God really
wants us to answer for ourselves and for him—that *this*,
after all, despite all, and above all, is what counts most with
him.

More than these! Do you love me more than these? The
ready forgiveness of God is implied in this question, but
also implied is that he expects something more of us than
the *status quo ante*. The "these" to which the question
refers were the fish, the nets, the boats—life as usual. Peter
realized, I think, that it was a subtle betrayal of his Lord
all over again to go back to fishing for fish. His previous
betrayal was that of mortal terror in the face of immediate
personal peril to life and limb, of which betrayal he
promptly repented. Going fishing was the calm and calculated betrayal of living as though nothing had happened to
him through his traveling with Jesus. How could business
be as usual after the resurrection? Nothing in life henceforth was "as usual," and Peter knew it very well. For
Peter, if he didn't love the Lord more than "these," he didn't
love the Lord.

Herein is confirmation of one of the basic facts of human
life and character. What we really are is determined by
what we really love. Human motivation is a terribly complex thing. Usually we act from a mixture of motives that
we ourselves cannot possibly sort out. Sometimes when our
behavior becomes too erratic, we need the help of a psy-
chiatrist to enable us to see why we behave as we do. All

manner of things play upon us, from inside us and from without, to shape our habit patterns, and ultimately our characters. Some of them we are aware of, and some we are not. Deep irrational fears and longings are a part of our make-up. Sometimes it is something from our half-remembered childhood that has given a peculiar twist to our subsequent behavior, without our realizing it. Furthermore, we are pushed and pulled a dozen different ways by the different persons whose opinions we value, and the different groups whose approval we covet. And behind them all are our genes—those mysterious carriers of the characteristics of our ancestry—which predispose us to a certain type of reaction. We are born with our particular body types, and other physical characteristics, that unquestionably have an influence upon our behavior. All these factors make up a complex of causes that no one can completely unravel. At worst they lead us to conclude that a man is a "pipe for fortune's finger to sound what stop she pleases." At best they lead us to be charitable in judging our neighbor's behavior at a given time and place. Certainly it should temper our harshness in judging Peter's defection from the Lord at the time of his need—and indeed in judging even Judas' betrayal. At least the disciples themselves had the grace to question each himself when Jesus announced that he would be betrayed by one of them. None was so sure of himself that he dared to question another. "Lord, is it I?"

But there is another factor, too, involved in our behavior and our character. It is, I believe, the most important one. It is what we love—or more particularly, whom we love. To whom do we respond? To whom do we give our attention? Whom do we want above all else to please? Whose smile is our greatest reward; whose frown our severest punishment? Who awakes in us our best, and subdues in us our worst? Who shapes our sense of values to his own? Who captures our wills until we want for ourselves what he wants for us? Love can be faked for a while. But someday the pretense will show up for what it is. Then a man's real love will be manifest—whether it be for money, or for fame, or for himself, or for whatever or whomever else. What a man loves above all else is within the realm of his personal freedom to determine, and it is the most important thing about him, whoever he is. This is confirmed in the fact that the first and great commandment is "Thou shalt love the Lord." It is confirmed, too, in that the first—indeed the only—question which the risen Christ demanded that Peter settle once for all, and which he alone could settle for himself, was "Simon, son of John, do *you* love *me?*" More than these—more than your opinions, your habits, your customary way of doing things, your comfort and your convenience. For all your failures of the past, your compromising involvements in the present—do you love me?

Notice how Peter answered. There was no braggadocio in him this time. There were no dramatic boasts, no impulsive vows. There was no effort to outdo his fellow disciples in parading his loyalty and courage. For Peter had learned. He knew himself too too well—perhaps he knew himself really for the first time. At least he knew what the real issue was. John Berryman, the poet, has observed that we moderns can live our entire lifetimes without ever finding out whether or not we are cowards. This comfortable evasion was not possible to Peter. He had found out. But he also knew where his heart was, or where he wanted it to be henceforth. Peter's reply was, "Yes, Lord, *you* know that I love you." He was aware that his fellow disciples may not have known that of him. He was sure that the public before whom he had so recently denied Jesus did not know it. But he knew, too, that the Christ who could read men's hearts and see what was inside of them could not be evaded or fooled. He could see what was hidden—whether it be of the good and the beautiful, or of ugliness and sin. From this awareness Peter rallied all that was in him of his affections and loyalty, and brought them to the one who had won them once and waited to do so again forever. "Yes, Lord, you know that I love you."

The divine reply was, "Feed my sheep." Simple, isn't it? No time or effort was to be spent in atonement, restitution, apology, or remorse. Peter was simply to start then and there to continue and extend the work of the good shepherd. He was to devote himself to the things that edify, build up, and nourish a hungry humanity. He was to do the things and support the things in this world that help people grow and that keep them healthy. He was to break the bread of life to a famished world. Once while riding on a night train, I learned that the colored man in the seat beside me was also a pastor, and we soon fell to discussing our common work. With great passion this devoted minister referred to this intercourse between Peter and the risen Lord at daybreak by the Sea of Galilee. "The Lord told Peter to feed his sheep," this latter-day shepherd reminded me. "He didn't say, 'fleece my sheep,' nor 'shear my sheep,' nor 'slaughter my sheep.' He said, 'feed my sheep, and tend my lambs.'"

These options are open to every man whether his vocation is in professional Christian service or not. No one who loves the Lord can remain in work that fleeces his sheep, or shears them, when there are so many ways in which men need to be fed, nourished, taught, healed, and tended. And if the work by which one earns his living seems remote from Christ's instructions to those who love him, he can participate indirectly through his avocation. The vast and varied Christian enterprise of mission cries out for his support. When Peter was commanded to continue the work of the good shepherd, there was no way open to him but to undertake it personally. He himself had to begin a person to person work of helping, teaching, preaching, healing, and that is what he did. This way is still open to every man who loves the Lord. But in addition, there are ways by which his reach can be lengthened until he is able to be at the sorest spots of human need on several continents simultaneously. For Christian missions are there. They are there with schools, hospitals, churches, and agricultural stations. The man who really loves the Lord will be there too through his support of this work—not in gesture and token, but in substantial sacrifice.

A few years ago, Dale Fiers, who heads the mission board of the Disciples of Christ, made a journey around the world to see the Christian work supervised by the board of which he is president. In the Belgian Congo he visited the Medical Evangelical Institute at Kimpese which several Christian communions support jointly. The Institute will train native nurses, technical assistants, and perhaps even physicians eventually, for the new civilizations now emerging in the Congo. While Fiers was visiting with an orthopedic surgeon on the staff there, the physician, Dr. Ernest Price, was summoned to the operating room. A young African boy had been run over by a truck, and had been brought to the hospital with the bones in his leg badly shattered and coming out through the flesh. Dr. Price worked for more than three hours to piece the leg back together, and succeeded so that the boy will walk again.[1]

This incident symbolizes profoundly what it means to "feed my sheep, and tend my lambs," in our twentieth century world. The truck represents the invasion of Western civilization into the ancient ways of the African. Perhaps it was a commercial vehicle, perhaps it was military. Its purpose may or may not have been beneficent. The injury was surely an accident, but in any event the African boy was its broken victim. Thank God that on that same spot the Church was present to bring to that same victim the compassion of the Christian part of Western civilization. And the Church was there because of some latter-day disciples who, for all their betrayals and failures, nevertheless love the Lord.

During his earthly life Jesus had told a parable that must surely have come back to Peter's mind during that breakfast on the beach. The parable told of the last judgment in which the King shall say to some of those before him, "I was hungry and you gave me food, I was thirsty and you

[1] A. Dale Fiers, *This Is Missions* (St. Louis: The Bethany Press, 1953), p. 63.

gave me drink, I was a stranger and you welcomed me, I was naked and you clothed me, I was sick and you visited me, I was in prison and you came to me." When the surprised hearers inquire when they had ever done these things for their Lord, he shall answer, "As you did it to one of the least of these my brethren, you did it to me" (Matt. 25:40). It is not strange that the one who spoke these words while in the flesh should continue to search the consciences of those who hear his name today, saying, "Do you love me? Then feed my sheep."

CHAPTER 13

Why Do You Persecute Me?

*At midday, O king, I saw on the way a light
from heaven, brighter than the sun, shining
round me and those who journeyed with me.
And when we had all fallen to the ground, I
heard a voice saying to me in the Hebrew
language, "Saul, Saul, why do you persecute
me? It hurts you to kick against the goads."
And I said, "Who are you, Lord?" And the
Lord said, "I am Jesus whom you are persecuting. But rise and stand upon your feet; for I
have appeared to you for this purpose, to
appoint you to serve and bear witness to the
things in which you have seen me and to those
in which I will appear to you."*

(Acts 26:13-16)

It is strange that Chris-
tianity's worst enemy later became its greatest champion.
It is remarkable that a Jewish rabbi became a Christian
missionary—and to Gentiles at that. It is surprising that a
legalist of the first water was later accused of being a
libertine. And it is strangest of all that a persecutor of the

cruelest stripe later endured martyrdom in the very cause he had been persecuting. Yet this is precisely what happened to Saul of Tarsus.

Saul "made havoc" of the Christian church that was in Jerusalem (Acts 9:21). "I persecuted the church of God violently, and tried to destroy it," was his own confession (Gal. 1:13). We are told that he "breathed threats and murder against the disciples of the Lord" (Acts 9:1). He went to the high priest of Judaism to get permission to chase, clear to Damascus, those Christians who had escaped him in Jerusalem. He intended to extradite them to Jerusalem, and to see to it that they were punished there. Paul had been present when Stephen was stoned to death, and had given his approval to it. He had even held the coats of those who had actually thrown the stones. (Acts 22:20.)

This latter event had unquestionably had a profound effect upon Saul. It got under his skin, deeply. Saul was not a bad man; he was a mistaken good one. He was a Pharisee with a tremendous zeal for God. Unquestionably he was a legalist and a fanatic. But he wasn't a mean or callous person. He persecuted Christians because he considered them to be the enemies of God himself. He thought in all honesty that they deserved nothing less than capital punishment, and had participated in it himself—at least to the extent of assisting at Stephen's execution.

Stephen had died as his master had died—seeking God's forgiveness for those who were even then killing him. "Lord, do not hold this sin against them," were among the last words he had the strength to speak (Acts 7:60). "Them" in this case included Saul. Here Saul—who con-

sidered himself to be a man of God, and who was so—
heard himself being prayed for, to the same God, by an
"infidel" whom he, Saul, was at that moment helping to
kill! Probably several other Christians whom he had
severely persecuted had displayed this same spirit. So Saul
intensified his efforts against all Christians. He lashed out
with all the blind fury of a man no longer sure of his
ground.

This was the purpose of the trip to Damascus. Saul was
chasing Christians into another country to bring them back
for punishment. But on this trip the event occurred which
changed the course of his entire life. Later, in describing
before King Herod Agrippa what had happened, Paul (as
Saul became known) gave this account: "At midday, O
king, I saw on the way a light from heaven, brighter than
the sun, shining round me and those who journeyed with
me. And when we had all fallen to the ground, I heard a
voice saying to me in the Hebrew language, 'Saul, Saul,
why do you persecute me? It hurts you to kick against the
goads.' And I said, 'Who are you, Lord?' And the Lord
said, 'I am Jesus whom you are persecuting. But rise and
stand upon your feet; for I have appeared to you for this
purpose, to appoint you to serve and bear witness.' "

This divine inquiry wrought in Saul of Tarsus the incredible changes we have noted. Time and again, Paul put
his finger upon this experience as the turning point of his
life. And it was. However we may explain it, however
many causes we may be able to detect leading up to it,
however many influences we may discern operating after it
to make Paul a Christian—this experience on the road to

Damascus was the decisive event in this man's life. And the insight which came to him then, whether formulated as a question or not, has changed other lives too. Not many, fortunately, have had experiences even remotely resembling Paul's traumatic shock on the Damascus road. But many people *have* seen a light under the impact of the question, "Why do you fight against God when it is hurting you so?" Surely it is an inquiry from God himself, however or by whomever it is voiced.

Notice how Paul heard the question. He was not asked why he had persecuted Stephen. Nor was he asked why he had been making life miserable for the disciples. He was asked, "Why do you persecute *me?*" "Who are you," Paul asked. "I am Jesus whom you are persecuting," came the reply. Now Paul, as well he knew, had been persecuting the *church.* Yet it now emerged in his awareness as an offense against—indeed as inflicting pain upon—the living Lord. And the church appeared to him as a divine enterprise in which Deity itself dwells, and acts, and feels. The implications of this event are startling to us as to Paul, but they are unmistakably there, and difficult to evade—that Jesus lives on in his church, that it is the continuation of his life on earth. Indeed, Paul spelled this idea out later in considerable anatomical detail when he called the church the body of Christ. (I Cor. 12:12-27.) It is metaphor, of course, but one so apt and precise that it is not far from reality itself. The church is the vehicle of Christ's spirit. It is the organism of which he is the mind. It is the extension of his life among men. This concept was so vivid to Paul that he frequently used the words church and Christ synonymously and interchangeably. The concept sets the mind racing from one vision to another. God meant Christ to dwell awhile in a human body. He also meant Christ to dwell forever in a corporate body that spans the earth and never dies. Can it be that the living Christ and the Christian Church are one and the same thing? And that you and I may be parts of him?

By this time the perceptive secular mind will have balked, and the sensitive Christian mind will have cringed. "This congregation of ours is Christ?" we ask in horror. Us? With our members—closer as we are to paganism than sainthood, and with our difficulties in getting along with each other? It has been truly observed that:

> To live with the saints in heaven
> Is bliss and glory.
> To live with the saints on earth
> Is often another story.

Are we to believe that that sectarian outfit up the street is Christ? That monstrous institution with all its robes, gold, machinery, medieval pageantry, and pompous falderal, is Christ? This is too much for reverent and honest minds to bear.

The idea made Paul shudder too. It tore him inside when quarrels, divisions, and worldliness crept into the church, as they did even during his lifetime. "Is Christ divided?" Paul cried in anguish to the Corinthian church when he learned that there were factions in it. (I Cor. 1:10-13.) Halford Luccock tells that when the United Church of Canada was in process of formation, a questionnaire was sent out to ministers in the western provinces to acquire information needed by the uniting churches. One question was, "What are the chief obstacles to religion in your community?" To this question one minister replied, "The chief obstacles to true religion in our community are whisky and the Methodists." But division is not the only shortcoming of the church as we know it. In the nineteenth century, William Dean Howells drew a picture of the church in a new England village in its subtle sell-out to the world. It sounds as though it might have been written of many of our twentieth century churches in city, town, and suburb.

Religion there had largely ceased to be a fact of spiritual experience, and the visible church flourished on condition of providing for the social needs of the community. It was practically held that the salvation of one's soul must not be made too depressing, or the young people would have nothing to do with it. Professors of the sternest creeds temporized with the sinners, and did what might be done to win them to heaven by helping them to have a good time here. The church embraced and included the world.[1]

Let us never be blind to the glaring faults of the church as we know it in our world.

But let us not overlook its holy nature either. Let us bear inside us the awful tension of the church as it is in ideal and essence, and the churches as they are in weakness and in fact. A gathering of sinners—the body of Christ—both

[1] *A Modern Instance* (Boston: Houghton Mifflin Co., 1881), p. 27.

are true of her. When Saul persecuted the first-century church with all its human faults and foibles, it was Christ who cried out, "Why do you persecute *me?*"

"It hurts you to kick against the goads" was the rest of God's breakthrough into the mind of Saul. To kick against the goads was a phrase current in both Latin and Greek languages meaning to fight against the will of the gods. To Paul, a good Jew and monotheist, this meant, of course, to fight against the will of God. It referred, in the stricken man's conscience, to his continuing on his own course with stubborn pride. It meant persisting in a pattern which God obviously wanted changed. It meant to resist further this fresh approach which God was making into human history and the hearts of men. It meant trying to undo what God had done, was doing, and meant to do. Now this sort of resistance is usually painful in itself. It brings frustration upon us. It brings doubts, and regrets, and inner conflicts to a person who has any religious sensitivities at all. Paul knew from his own raw conscience the pain of kicking against the goads, but he was a wonderfully stubborn man. And so—to put the matter in theological perspective, if not theological terminology—God finally had to clobber him.

I do believe that God intends to create for himself a people. Israel wouldn't do. So he created a new Israel in Jesus Christ, and included Gentiles. It was in resisting the beginnings of that development that Paul got hurt before he came around. I do believe that God intends to continue the creation of a people for himself in Jesus Christ that is ultimately to include all people who will allow themselves to be included. By it he will shatter the walls which we build between ourselves and our neighbors, just as he shattered the walls between Jew and Gentile in Paul's day, thus making new creatures of us all. After observing that "Rome had made a solitude, and called it peace," C. H. Dodd continues: "There is nothing which in the last resort can unite mankind but the free contagion of this life. . . . Man is born to be a son of God, and only in 'the liberty of the splendor of the sons of God' can the commonwealth of man be founded." [2] That is what I believe the church means—what it is all about. I believe that through it God intends to bring all men together unto himself as sons, and unto each other as brothers, and that if men in the church or outside of it stand in the way, someone is going to get hurt.

Sometimes this divine vision emerges, imperfectly and temporarily, but clear enough so that we can see it with our own eyes, in the here and now. And when it does, it is a shaking experience. When the all-Negro cast of George Gershwin's folk opera *Porgy and Bess* were on tour in Russia several years ago, eleven of the members attended morning worship in the Baptist Evangelical Church in Leningrad on Christmas Day. Among them was Rhoda Boggs who played the role of the strawberry woman in the opera. Truman Capote, who wrote of this tour, tells of returning to the Astoria Hotel, and seeing the actress sitting at a table sobbing. He inquired what was the matter.

She told him,

[2] *The Meaning of Paul for To-Day* (New York: George H. Doran, 1920), pp. 47-48.

Why Do You Persecute Me?

I'm tore to pieces. I've been going to church since I can walk, but I never felt Jesus like I felt Jesus today. Oh, child, he was *there*. He was out in the open. He was plainly written on every face. He was singing with us, and you never heard such beautiful singing. It was old people mostly, and old people can't sing like that without Jesus is helping them along. The pastor asked us colored people would we render a spiritual, and they listened so quiet, all those rows and rows and rows of old faces just looking at us, like we were telling them nobody's alone when Jesus is everywhere on this earth, which is a fact they know already, but it seemed to me like they were glad to hear about it. Anybody doubts the presence of Our Saviour, he should've been there. Well, it came time to go. And you know what happened? They stood up the whole congregation. They took out white handkerchiefs and waved them in the air. And they sang, "God Be with You Till We Meet Again." The tears were just pouring down our faces, them and ours. Oh, child, it churned me up.[3]

When we attend our own services of worship as worshipers, we may subconsciously tend to regard the services as a sort of theatrical production. In such a scheme, the minister and the choir are the performers. God (it is presumed) is behind the scenes as a prompter. And the congregation is the audience which watches and judges the performance. Not so, not so, said Kierkegaard. In genuine Christian worship, the congregation are the actors. The minister is merely the prompter—and the audience which watches and judges the whole performance is God him-

[3] *The Muses Are Heard*, copyright 1956 by Truman Capote. Reprinted by permission of Random House, Inc.

self. In one of his letters Paul said of Christ that "He is before all things, and in him *all things hold together*. He is the head of the body, the church; he is the beginning, the firstborn from the dead, that in everything he might be pre-eminent. For *in* him all the fullness of God was pleased to dwell, and *through* him to *reconcile to himself all things*." That is the plot.